The Inventive Yankee

The Inventive Yankee

From rockets to roller skates,
200 years of Yankee inventors & inventions.

YANKEE BOOKS

Camden, Maine

Staff for this book:
Editor: Andrea Chesman
Designer: Eugenie Seidenberg-Delaney
Photo Editor: Jamie Kageleiry
Yankee Publishing Incorporated
Dublin, New Hampshire 03444

COVER PHOTO CREDITS

1. RI Red rooster: courtesy RI Division of Agriculture
2. Silly Putty Egg: Binney & Smith Incorporated, Easton, PA
3. Diving mask: courtesy Mike Ambrose, Undersea Divers, Beverly, MA
4. Rocket: courtesy Chad Kageleiry
5. Sewing machine: courtesy Fran Kageleiry
6. Polaroid camera: courtesy Jack Naylor
7. Bowling pin: courtesy Dover Bowl, Dover, NH
8. Parker House roll: Harvey's Bakery, Dover, NH
9. Catcher's mitt: courtesy Evelyn Mamigarian
10. Earmuffs: courtesy C. R. Tyler
11. Fannie Farmer Cookbook: courtesy Jacqueline Guilmette
12. Axe: courtesy Chad Kageleiry
13. Lizzie Borden photo: Culver Pictures, Inc.
14. Wiffle Ball: The Wiffle Ball Company, Shelton, CT.
15. Roller skate: courtesy Priscilla Smith

First Edition
Copyright ©1989 by Yankee Publishing Incorporated

Library of Congress Cataloging-in-Publication Data

The Inventive Yankee.
    Includes index.
    1. Inventors — New England — Biography. I. Yankee
Books.
T39.I58   1989   609.2'2 [B]   88-33893
ISBN 0-89909-172-5
Second Printing, 1990

CONTENTS

INTRODUCTION

In 1641, the Massachusetts General Court granted a process patent to Samuel Winslow for a novel method of producing salt. It was the first patent on the new continent, and it instigated nearly 350 years of Yankee ingenuity. That is what this book is all about: the collective inventive mind of a region.

Let's face it, genius of one sort or another is a New England hallmark. We're not bragging; Yankees are tinkerers at heart. Years ago, the New England farmer was admired for his short cuts around the barnyard. Put a Yankee in the Garden of Eden, Josh Billings once wrote, ". . . and he would see where he could alter it to advantage. . . ." As a phrase, "Yankee ingenuity," like Kleenex or Dixie Cup (invented in New England, by the way), is so pervasive it serves as the generic symbol for a nation's creative affinity for progress.

Mark Twain understood Yankee ingenuity better than any other writer. A converted Yankee, Twain invested his fortune in a series of inventive disasters, including a typesetting device that revolutionized Twain's bank statement but not much else. "I am a Yankee of the Yankees — and practical," Twain wrote in *A Connecticut Yankee in King Arthur's Court.* "Why I could make anything a body wanted — anything in the world, it didn't make any difference what; and if there wasn't any quick new-fangled way to make a thing, I could invent one — and do it as easy as rolling off a log."

An inventor himself, Twain was issued three patents, including one for a blank, self-pasting scrapbook, prompting at least one literary critic to dub it Twain's greatest work.

Representatives from other regions of the country, jealous no doubt, might argue that New Englanders lead the nation in innovations of one sort or another primarily because we were here first. Had the Pilgrims dropped anchor at Plymouth Rock, then hightailed it straight through the interior to, say, Ohio, maybe the creative light would have flickered first in the Midwest. "Buckeye ingenuity," they might suggest, would then be the watchword for anything new, different, or simply amazing.

Well, maybe? Maybe not! As any good prosecuting attorney would say, the facts speak for themselves. Consider that of the fifty-eight inventors in the National Inventors Hall of Fame located in Arlington, Virginia, twelve are either native to the region or completed their research here. New England saw the development of the horseless carriage, the snow shovel, the snowmobile, the rope tow, the helicopter and the rocket; frozen food, fried clams, and the microwave oven; the artificial lung, the pacemaker, and the birth control pill. The list is as rich and quirky as the agenda of a town meeting.

Since invention and patenting go hand in hand, it should come as no surprise that Benjamin Huntington, a representative from Connecticut, helped prepare the first patent office proposal to Congress on February 16, 1790. Or that Samuel Hopkins of Pittsford, Vermont, was issued the first U.S. patent for a new process to produce pot ash. The first woman to receive a patent was also a Yankee: In 1809, Mary Kies, of Killingly, Connecticut, invented a method of weaving straw with silk and thread.

The modern U.S. Patent Office, the world's model of how a patent department should be run, was reorganized by John Ruggles, an inventor and senator from Maine. On July 4, 1836, Congress enacted the patent search, the invention model, and the requirement to prove both novelty and utility in invention. Ruggles was issued patent #1, from which all subsequent patents are numbered, for a locomotive steam engine ". . . to prevent the evil of the sliding of the wheels [of the locomotive]."

The list of important, influential, and absolutely essential Yankee contributions could go on and on (it's a little like standing at the ice cream counter, choosing among thirty-two flavors: They all look good). But you get the point.

Genius is not simply defined by mechanical invention or resounding success. The region has produced noteworthy flops, such as Langley's airplane and Roper's one and only ride on a steam bicycle, and creative scoundrels such as Henry Tufts, Lizzie Borden, and the Brink's gang, whose millions are still unaccounted for. "The genius of New England," says *Yankee* magazine editor Judson D. Hale, Sr., a notable Yankee in his own right, "is that essential spirit or nature of each state, combined as both the myth and the reality of our beloved region as a whole. It is everywhere within us all."

CHAPTER ONE

The Sons of Eli

*Or How the Cotton Gin
Led to the Computer*

What Else Did Eli Whitney Do?

Well, he made guns, for one thing, and in the process developed what we all consider to be a twentieth-century concept — the assembly line.

In 1794, Eli Whitney, a resident of New Haven, Connecticut, hit upon the basic concepts of the cotton gin and successfully produced a machine that drastically changed the way of life in the South. Perhaps a fact not so well known is that Whitney's boon to the cotton industry almost became his Armageddon.

Patent infringements forced him to bring scores of lawsuits, which drained him emotionally and financially. Even when he prevailed in a suit and collected damages, legal fees chewed up the award and more.

Disgusted with the fight to make the ginning business profitable, Whitney looked to other endeavors. At the time, war with France seemed likely, and it was equally clear that the United States could no longer depend on imported arms for its defense. However, the industrial capacity of the fledgling nation was still limited.

This was a time when firearms were made start to finish by one gunsmith. Parts were hand fitted to make each gun function, and production was painstakingly slow. A new armory at Springfield, Massachusetts, was able to complete only about 245 muskets in the first year of its operation. The new nation needed tens of thousands of arms.

Sensing this need, Whitney decided to meet it by proposing to produce ten thousand muskets in just two years! He also proposed that the parts of one musket lock would fit any of the ten thousand musket locks. The topper was that Eli Whitney had never built a musket in his life.

An ancient mill site at the base of East Rock presented a perfect location for the erection of a factory. The swiftly moving Mill River provided a ready source of power. Labor shortages and severe weather caused construction delays, but eventually, the building was completed and large quantities of tools, mill irons, charcoal, and rolled iron rods began to arrive, much to the surprise of the townspeople. Whitney's plan, commonplace today, was to have all the materials needed to make ten thousand muskets on hand before he began. In 1799, this wasn't understood by other manufacturers, let alone the general public.

Whitney began with a simple jig for filing triggers and hammers. The unskilled workman would place the rough piece into the jig and file it to the required shape. Since the jig prevented errors, the workman could repeat this simple act again and again. Another individual would

This engraving from a portrait of Eli Whitney was done by Samuel F. B. Morse, another famous inventor, c. 1822.

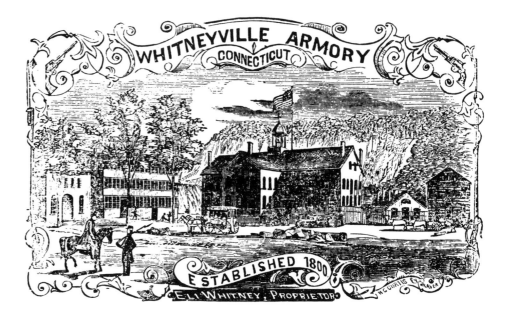

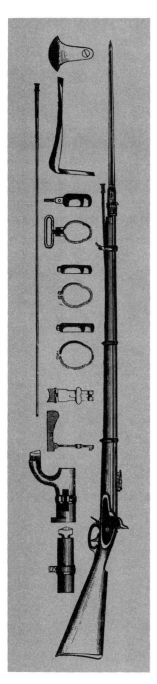

Whitney's contribution was the concept of division of labor. At his armory (right), he was the first to build muskets with interchangeable parts. Shown above, an Enfield rifle with interchangeable parts.

work on an entirely different operation using special tools created for that job. Whitney had developed the concept of division of labor as no one else before him had. No longer would a musket be built by one man, and a gun could be completed in a matter of days when the system was rolling under full steam.

The guns themselves were based on the French Charleville model of 1763, a long, graceful arm with a flintlock ignition system. When the trigger was pulled, the flint, which was clamped between the maws of the hammer, struck a steel plate called a frizzen, which sent a shower of sparks into a pan filled with fine powder. This priming powder burned rapidly, setting off the main charge in the gun barrel. The guns were, of course, muzzle loaded and single shot. At this time the methods of warfare still stressed the bayonet as a major weapon. The plan of attack usually called for the infantry to fire one or two volleys and then to close in on the enemy as soon as possible. These early French weapons frequently misfired and were not particularly accurate. Often the priming powder would flash but would not set off the main charge; hence, the term to describe a type of individual — a "flash in the pan."

Whitney developed an improved pan that insured more consistent ignition and also helped to keep the powder dry. These improved muskets were of excellent quality, but the rate of production couldn't meet the contract terms. Whitney was forced to ask for extensions.

Whitney's critics, some sincere and others jealous, severely questioned his request. To blunt the criticism, Whitney went to Washington to provide a practical demonstration for the critics and some allies, including Thomas Jefferson and President Adams. This part of the story of Whitney's guns is well known. He literally dumped the parts of ten gun locks on a table and challenged the men to assemble them, choosing from any of the parts. Although the group was skeptical at first, the men soon discovered that Whitney's idea for interchangeable parts really worked. Adams was satisfied, Jefferson again impressed, and the others were silenced. The contract extension was granted.

That proved to be a blessing, because Whitney wasn't able to complete the original order until 1808. It had taken him ten years instead of the promised two — but manufacturing would never again be the same.

The Electric Motor:
Forerunner of Today's Appliances and Tools

Thomas Davenport

By all accounts, Thomas Davenport, a blacksmith from Brandon, Vermont, was a decent, hard-working fellow until he saw an electromagnet. From then on, he became obsessed with unleashing its potential. The first rotary electric motor — his contribution to technology — was the forerunner of the motor that today drives most household appliances and tools.

Davenport was the fourth of eleven children born to a poor family in Williamstown, Vermont. At the age of fourteen, with only three years of schooling, he was apprenticed to a blacksmith and later opened his own shop.

In 1831, Davenport visited the Penfield Iron Works in upstate New York, where Joseph Henry, the dean of American scientists of his day, had installed the first commercial electromagnet. Capable of lifting an amazing weight of 750 pounds, it was used to extract iron from pulverized ore. Davenport wondered what would happen if the wire ends of the magnet were broken and then placed back together again: Would the current pass through once more? The answer, he was told, was no.

The blacksmith had to see for himself. To purchase his own electromagnet, he sold his brother's horse for an inferior nag and some cash. He then fabricated a second magnet, using his wife's silk wedding dress to insulate the wires. He mounted the pair on a wheel and connected them to a battery for power. By alternating the current from one magnet to the other, the wheel turned. Davenport used the invention to drive his own drills and wood-turning lathe.

Luck was never on his side. In 1836, he set out on foot for the Patent Office in Washington, D.C., demonstrating his invention along the way. By the time he reached the capital, he had squandered the application

A model of the Davenport motor, now in the Smithsonian Institution.

money, and so he returned to Vermont empty handed. When he finally raised the necessary capital and mailed in his application, the Patent Office was destroyed in a fire. He finally received credit for his device on February 5, 1837.

Credit was all Davenport would ever receive. Described by one historian as "a brilliantly unsuccessful inventor," Davenport also invented the electric railway, the electric piano, the electric trolley, the electric printing press, and a version of the electric telegraph. All of his inventions relied on the rotating motor, but the batteries used to drive the motors were too heavy, fragile, and costly for any practical commercial use. Another fifty years would pass before the potential of the electric motor was fully realized. According to his sons, Thomas Davenport died in 1851 of a broken heart at the age of forty-one, when Samuel Morse and not he was credited with inventing the telegraph.

A Revolution in Bridge Design

The American contribution to railroading for the masses was in the art of the inexpensive railway. Like the telephone and the telegraph, the railroad connected the country. Between 1830 and 1890, 250,000 miles of railroad track were laid each year. None of it could have occurred without the Howe truss, a bridge support patented by William Howe of Spencer, Massachusetts, uncle to the inventor of the sewing machine.

There were truss designs prior to Howe's that derived their strength from a lattice of triangular shapes underneath the bridge bed. The first of these was patented in 1820 by Ithiel Town, an architect from New Haven, Connecticut. Town charged one dollar a foot for every bridge built by a license under his patent, two dollars a foot whenever he found one built without his permission. In spite of the cost, it was a popular design for several decades. But in 1840, the Town design proved dramatically inadequate for the increasing weight of locomotives when one of his bridges over Catskill Creek in New York State collapsed, killing a workman. It was the first railroad bridge fatality in the country.

That same year Howe introduced his much simpler design. The secret to the Howe truss was the introduction of wrought-iron rods as vertical tension members running all the way through the top and bottom chords. Nuts attached to their threaded ends could be tightened from time to time.

This last touch solved another problem that had cropped up only

recently. With the frantic pace of rail building, cured timbers had become a scarce commodity. With its adjustable nuts, the Howe truss could accommodate the shrinking and checking that occurred as green lumber cured. The Howe design had only one real drawback — the timbers often caught on fire.

In the 1860s, wood gave way to all-iron bridges. The first of these using a Howe design was built in 1865 at Ashtabula, Ohio, to carry the Lake Shore Railway over a steep gorge near Lake Erie. Eleven years later, it collapsed, carrying more than eighty people to their deaths in the ravine below. This disaster foreshadowed a ten-year period of bridge failure, when as many as twenty-five iron bridges a year collapsed. The reason for the failure was later determined to be due to the nature of wrought iron under tension, not the design. Iron was replaced by steel, and the Howe truss design persisted well into the next century.

Above: *The doomed Lake Shore Railroad Bridge near Ashtabula, Ohio, built in 1865. Next page: Three men on a log using peavey bars.*

Peavey Lost the Patent But Won Immortality

One afternoon in the spring of 1858, Joseph Peavey, a blacksmith from Stillwater Village near Bangor, Maine, lay on his stomach on a covered bridge that crossed the Stillwater branch of the Penobscot River. Through a crack in the floor, he watched a crew of rivermen trying

Joseph Peavey

13

THE LOG SKIDDER

The logging skidder was invented by Elijah "Tiger" White, best known as the oldest stock car racer at the Oxford Plains Speedway in Carthage, Maine. In the 1940s, White and his brothers Ervin and Hurchial formed the White Brothers logging company. Wanting something better to use for skidding logs from the woods than their old crawler tractor, they modified a 1929 four-wheel-drive FWD truck with spare parts lying around the yard. Their rubber-wheeled creation manuevered so well in all terrain that rival loggers nicknamed the machine "Muscles." The Whites never bothered to patent "Muscles" — they were loggers, they explained, not manufacturers, and happy with life as they found it. The FWD Truck Company, however, copied the skidder, patented it, and in the early 1950s introduced the "Blue Ox." It did not sell, which came as no surprise to Tiger White. "Engineers made it," he explained. "We put our machine together so we could use it. They looked at our machine and thought it needed to be improved."

to break up a log jam.

As Peavey watched in amusement, he was struck with a solution to their problem. Returning immediately to his shop, he and his son Daniel adapted a cant-dog by making a rigid clasp to encircle the staff, with lips on one side. The lips were drilled to take a bolt that would hold a hook, or dog, in place, allowing it to move up and down but not sideways. Below the bulge in the handle, Daniel placed graduated collars of iron which added greatly to the strength of the handle. Then Peavey drove a sharp iron spike into the end of the rig.

The resulting cant-dog looked like some medieval weapon, but the peavey bar, as it came to be called, was a triumph of design mated to application. William Hale, a noted river boss, pronounced it the soundest tool ever put into the hands of a woodsman. Peavey, assuming fame and fortune were soon to follow, drew a model of his invention and set out on foot for the Bangor post office, patent application in hand.

Along the way, he stopped in Orono to visit with another blacksmith. The pair had a drink together, then another and another. In that chummy atmosphere, Peavey revealed his plans for the cant-dog. When he awoke in the morning, somewhat hungover, he discovered that his drawings and an application for a "Patent Cant-dog" were on their way to Washington, submitted by the Orono blacksmith.

While the peavey bar was not patented under the blacksmith's name, his name was immortalized. The Peavey family manufactured the peavey bars most widely used, and the peavey bar became the generic term applied to all cant-dogs. For many years the family factory in Brewer sported a ten-foot sign above the door with just two letters, one at each end: P V. The Peavey headstone in the Bangor cemetery bears a large letter P crossed by two carved peaveys.

14

Goodyear's Accident

Charles Goodyear

Charles Goodyear may not have coined the expression "rubber check," but it certainly applied to the inventor of the process for vulcanizing rubber, who died a pauper, hounded by collection agents.

Born in 1800, Goodyear was the son of an entrepreneur and inventor who manufactured hardware at his factory in New Haven, Connecticut. Though he once studied for the ministry, Goodyear moved to Philadelphia in 1826 and opened the first hardware store stocked exclusively with American-made goods. It was here that his woes began. At the age of thirty, his health and business declined. Hopelessly in debt, Goodyear was forced to sell the store. While the business later flourished under new management, he spent the next ten years in and out of debtor's prison.

In 1834, during one of his spells as a free man, Goodyear purchased a life preserver from the Roxbury India Rubber Company in New York. Suffering from the inventor's predilection to improvise, Goodyear tinkered with the inner tube, then returned the improved model to the company store. Admiring his work, the rubber manufacturers told him their saga: The company was on the brink of financial ruin; during the previous year, twenty thousand dollars worth of spoiled goods had been returned. In hot weather, it seemed, rubber melted, and in cold weather it petrified. The individual who could unlock the secret to India rubber, Goodyear was assured, stood to make a fortune.

A photo from the early 1900s shows workers applying treads to Goodyear tires.

The 55,555,555th Goodyear cord tire, which rolled off the Akron, Ohio, assembly line on October 4, 1923.

To someone forever in debt, these words were like throwing a life preserver to a drowning man. The raw material was cheap, and the necessary equipment for experimenting with rubber could be found in his wife's kitchen: a rolling pin, a marble slab, and a few pots and pans. Vulcanizing rubber (improving its strength and resiliency) became Goodyear's mission in life. He worked at home in New Haven and at a workshop in Greenwich Village, where he often passed out from the fumes. Only the generosity of friends and family kept him alive. Since he was frequently in prison, he continued his experiments behind bars. A friend described Goodyear's financial predicament: "If you meet a man who has on an India rubber cap, stock, coat, vest, and shoes, with an India rubber money purse without a cent of money in it, that is he."

In 1839, Goodyear's fortunes appeared as if they were about to turn for the better. Buoyed by an experiment combining rubber with sulfur, he took a government order for rubber mailbags. Though the mailbags fell to pieces, Goodyear thought he was on the right track. According to legend, as he was boiling a fresh batch of rubber and sulfur in his brother-in-law's kitchen in Woburn, Massachusetts, Goodyear accidentally dropped a blob on the stove. After it cooled, the vulcanized rubber was hard and firm, yet pliable.

Success still eluded Goodyear. He had worn out his welcome with potential backers, and another five years passed before he was able to patent the process. By then, his rights were challenged, and his products pirated. In 1852, Goodyear pleaded his case before the U.S. Circuit Court in Trenton, New Jersey. Daniel Webster, who was then secretary of state, represented the beleaguered inventor. Eloquent as ever, Webster prevailed in court, but Goodyear was never able to translate victory into capital. When he died in 1860, his estate was two hundred thousand dollars in arrears.

That Man Could Swim Like the Fish

M an has always sought to master the natural elements. While some taught us to fly like the birds, Leonard Norcross, inventor of the rubber diving suit, taught us to swim like the fish.

According to some reports, experiments in diving were conducted in Europe in the early 18th century. A Frenchman named Augustus Siebe is credited with developing a metal diving helmet in 1819 which he later developed into a full diving suit in 1837.

At the same time, Norcross, a mechanic and deacon of the Congregational Church, was working across the Atlantic on the same invention in the little town of Dixfield, Maine. He had already patented machines for making wrought-iron nails, dressing stone, and pulling stumps as early as 1830, when he began to create "submarine armor."

The cap was made of lead to cover the head and neck, with glass in the front. A lantern that swiveled on a pivot was placed on top. Air was pumped to the diver through a hose attached to the top of the cap, and a safety valve allowed for foul air to escape. In the earliest versions of submarine armor, Norcross used leather for the suit, later replaced by Goodyear's India rubber cloth.

In May of 1834, Norcross made his first descent from Brigadier Rock in the Webb River. According to one contemporary account, he was so elated by the successful dive that he went home and collapsed in his chair "in hearty laughter." After a second trial in Winthrop, Maine, Norcross was granted a patent on his rubber diving suit on June 14, 1834. He named one of his sons Submarinus in honor of his achievement.

To promote his invention, Norcross traveled across the country. The following September, he made a descent in Boston; in October, he received a silver medal for the diving suit at the Fair of the American Institute in New York. A Norcross-designed suit is said to have been used in the process of raising the Russian fleet after it was sunk in the harbor of Sebastapol and by those cleaning the bottoms of Union gunboats during the Civil War.

Though Norcross formed the U.S. Submarine Company, he received little benefit from his invention. Norcross died in his hometown of Dixfield on March 10, 1864.

Top: *The early deep-sea diving suits looked like something from the pages of a science-fiction comic book.* Bottom: *A diver grapples with an octopus.*

"What Hath God Wrought!"

What hath God wrought!" This Biblical portent (*Numbers 23:23*) was the first official message Samuel F. B. Morse transmitted by telegraph (the F. B. stood for Finley Breese, and the family called him Finley). While there is considerable debate as to who actually invented the telegraph, there is no question that Morse brought the world closer together and foreshadowed the invention of the telephone, radio, and television.

Born the son of a Congregational minister in Charlestown, Massachusetts, in 1791, Morse was a Yale-educated man with a chest-length beard. He passed the early portion of his life as a portrait painter in both Europe and the United States. One of his best-known portraits is of Eli Whitney. Morse also taught art at the University of the City of New York and once ran unsuccessfully for mayor of New York on the anti-Catholic, anti-immigrant, Native American ticket.

The idea that electromagnetic forces could carry signals a great distance in seconds was not Morse's. André Marie Ampère, a French physicist, performed some of the early experiments, and primitive telegraphs were developed in England in the 1830s by W. F. Cook and Charles Wheatstone, a medical student and a physicist. Joseph Henry, the dean of American electrical scientists who was later to become director of the Smithsonian Institution, developed an early version of the instrument.

Where others saw a scientific toy, Morse envisioned communication. His first contribution was the invention of the relay, which amplified a weak electrical impulse and allowed it to travel more than the then-typical forty-five feet. With his assistant Alfred Lewis Vail, Morse also devised a code of dots and dashes, though all patents carried only Morse's name. The earliest known message was "Successful experiment with telegraph. September 4th, 1837." Morse received patent #1,647 for "Telegraph Signs," or the Morse code, on June 20, 1840.

Morse's real contribution to the advancement of the telegraph was in his tenacity to seek federal funding for the invention. Political forces, including Postmaster General Johnson, who feared the telegraph would rival his Post Office Department, bitterly opposed government spending on the telegraph. Morse petitioned Congress for several years before he was finally awarded thirty thousand dollars to construct a thirty-eight-mile telegraph line between Baltimore and Washington, from poles along the B&O right of way. On May 1, 1844, Vail tapped out the first breaking news story after he learned the Whigs in the national convention in Baltimore had just named Henry Clay and Theodore Frelinghuysen as their candidates for president and vice president: "The ticket is

Samuel F. B. Morse

Clay and Frelinghuysen." His message beat the returning delegates' train to Washington by sixty-four minutes. Morse formally demonstrated the telegraph on May 24, at ceremonies in the chamber of the Supreme Court. Ever politically astute, Morse had Annie Ellsworth, the daughter of the commissioner of patents, choose the first message to be transmitted.

Not everyone recognized the advantages of instantaneous communication. Some farmers, convinced that it disturbed the weather and ruined crops, tore down miles of telegraph wire. But by 1861, a coast-to-coast telegraph line was completed. Five years later, the first transatlantic telegraph cable was laid, and news that once took twelve days to cross the Atlantic by steamer completed the journey in minutes.

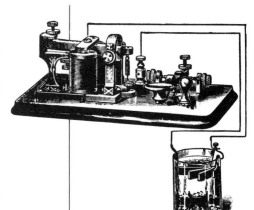

For just $3.50 in 1895, one could purchase from Montgomery Ward & Co. a learner's telegraph, complete with full size key and sounder, instruction book, and wire. Batteries included.

"I Can Hear You!"

The story of the invention of the telephone still fuels the imagination of every back-yard tinkerer who ever dreamed of changing history. The most valuable patent ever granted was the result of an accident. At the time, Alexander Graham Bell was only twenty-nine years old.

Bell was born into a family of famous speech teachers in Edinburgh, Scotland, in 1847. At the age of fifteen, he moved to London, where he soon found a position teaching elocution and music at a boarding school for young gentlemen. There he met Alexander J. Ellis, president of the London Philological Society, who demonstrated how tuning forks could be kept in vibration by electromagnets to imitate human vocal sounds. From those demonstrations, Bell got the idea for transmitting the human voice over a wire.

After contracting tuberculosis, he emigrated to Canada in 1870, where he achieved notable success in teaching deaf-mute children to speak. As his reputation spread, Bell was invited to open a school for the training of teachers of the deaf in Boston. In 1873, he became professor of vocal physiology and elocution at Boston University.

All the while, he continued to experiment with electrical communication from a workshop on Court Street in Boston with the backing of Gardiner Greene Hubbard, a prominent patent lawyer, and Thomas Sanders, a prosperous leather merchant.

The telephone was actually an afterthought. Neither Sanders nor Hubbard, who were footing the bill, thought much of the idea. Instead, they encouraged Bell to concentrate on the harmonic telegraph — a multiple-line telegraph that could receive and sort through a number of

Bell's first telephone.

19

MORE TELEPHONE FIRSTS

Yankee ingenuity and the telephone did not end with Bell. In 1877, William Gray, a Connecticut inventor, installed the first slot machine for pay telephone calls. A year later, the first commercial telephone exchange was established in New Haven, Connecticut, and Southern New England Telephone Company issued the first telephone directory for its new customers, a one-page edition. More recently, the PicTel Corporation of Peabody, Massachusetts, has patented a two-way picture telephone system that allows two people to see and hear each other on a color video display screen using regular telephone lines. "With our system it is just as good as being there, but you can't shake hands and buy someone lunch," Tom Spaulding, vice president of PicTel, commented in the *Boston Globe*.

messages at once. On the afternoon of June 2, 1875, Bell was in the receiving room, while his assistant, Thomas A. Watson, was in the transmitting room. The steel organ reeds used in the harmonic telegraph needed constant retuning by means of an adjustment screw, and when one of the reeds became stuck, Watson plucked at it again and again to free it.

In the room next door, Bell suddenly heard the sound of a plucked reed. "What did you do then?" he yelled to Watson. "Don't change anything. Let me see!" By sheer accident, the reed had become a diaphragm and transmitted sound.

Soon Watson and Bell had constructed a crude telephone that transmitted the faint murmur of Bell's voice. It wasn't until March 7, 1876, that patent #174,465 was issued for "Telegraphy." Three days later, on March 10, 1876, Bell cried out, "Mr. Watson, come here. I want you," after spilling battery acid on his trousers. The pair had strung wires down two flights of stairs, and Watson bounded up the steps. "I can hear you," he said. "I can hear the words!"

That summer, after listening to the telephone at the Centennial Exhibition in Philadelphia, Sir William Thompson predicted ". . . before long, friends will whisper their secrets over the electric wire." Five years later, Bell was worth about a million dollars, with an annual income of thirty-seven thousand dollars. In short order, his weight ballooned like his fortune from 165 to 250 pounds. Though he continued to invent up until his death in 1922 (his patronage resulted in the invention of the hydrofoil, and under his influence the magazine *Science* was founded in

1880), none of his future achievements would ever rival the phone.

Years later, Watson reflected on the first telephone call. "Perhaps if Mr. Bell had realized that he was about to make a bit of history," Watson said, "he would have been prepared with a more sounding and interesting sentence."

How to Beat a Cold Yankee Winter

On Christmas Day in 1873, Chester Greenwood received a pair of ice skates from his parents. From the look on the face of the fifteen-year-old boy from Farmington, Maine, one would have thought Greenwood had discovered a lump of coal in his stocking. He was concerned about his sensitive ears.

"If I go skating," Chester complained to his mother, "they'll start aching. They always ache when I'm out in the cold too long."

After some discussion, Greenwood's mother suggested Chester cover his ears with his hands while he skated. "They'll keep your ears warm," she assured him. Less than an hour after he left the house, Greenwood returned with blue ears. "My ears froze up on me as I was walking to the pond," he said. "I had to run all the way home."

The frustrated skater asked his mother to sew fur onto two ear-shaped loops of wire. Emily Greenwood followed her son's instructions, and in no time at all, Greenwood had hooked the wires onto a bowler hat. With the fur protecting his ears, he finally went back to the pond to skate.

Faster than you can say "earmuff," Mrs. Greenwood was devoting all of her spare time to the production of "Chester's ear protectors." First the neighbors wanted a pair; soon, local shopkeepers were selling them. Nearly four years later, on March 13, 1877, Greenwood was granted patent #188,292 for his invention. By that time he had improved the design with the addition of a spring that allowed the earmuffs to fit over the head and stay in place. To help his mother keep up with the orders, Greenwood hired extra hands and then invented a machine to produce the earmuffs in a factory. Greenwood's Champion Ear Protectors, or earlaps as they were also called, sold by the hundreds, the thousands, and finally the millions. In 1937, when Greenwood passed away at the age of seventy-nine, the factory was operating around the clock, and Farmington, Maine, had been transformed into the earmuff capital of the world.

Opposite page: *Bell opening the New York-Chicago long distance telephone line, 1892.*

Chester Greenwood

An early ad for Greenwood's ear muffs.

The Writing on the Wall

Credit Dr. Hall with the development of the blackboard, shown here in a Brookline, Vermont, schoolhouse, c. 1916.

Dr. Samuel Read Hall

If you can read this book, you probably owe a debt to the invention of the Reverend Samuel Read Hall, one of the country's earliest educators.

Born in Croydon, New Hampshire, in 1795, Hall began his teaching career at the age of eighteen in Rumford, Maine. In 1823, a year after he was ordained as a Congregational minister, Hall founded Concord Academy in Concord, Vermont, the first school in the United States for training teachers in the art of "school-keeping." That same year, Hall patented one of his teaching innovations, a pine board planed smooth and painted black — the blackboard.

The reverend went on to distinguish himself as an educator and clergyman in Andover, Massachusetts; Plymouth, New Hampshire; and Craftsbury, Vermont, where he often served as both teacher and Congregational minister. He is often credited with raising teaching from a primitive level to that of a scientifically trained profession. In 1829, he published *Lectures on School-Keeping,* the first American pedagogical textbook on teaching. More than ten thousand copies were sold, making it the *Gone with the Wind* of its day; many of his principles and methods are still used today.

In 1830, Hall was one of the founders of the American Institute of Instruction, one of the earliest educational associations in the country. That same year, he left Vermont to become principal of Phillips Andover Academy in Massachusetts. He died in Vermont on June 24, 1877. A stone shaft with a bronze tablet dedicated to Hall and the Concord Academy is located outside of Concord, Vermont.

They Said It Couldn't Be Done

Above: *The arrow piercing the name was Gillette's trademark. Below left: Drawings from Gillette's 1904 patent application. Below right: King Camp Gillette.*

King Camp Gillette, the man who popularized the safety razor, was never content with revolutionizing a morning ritual. The safety razor was just a way station on his path to streamlining the business of running the world.

Born in 1855 to a Chicago postman and the author of a best-selling cookbook, Gillette tossed around for years before finding his niche. He was a clerk in Chicago and sold scouring powder in Britain. In 1894, after marrying the daughter of an oil man, he published *The Human Drift,* which outlined his plan to incorporate the world. The book was as unsuccessful as the Twentieth Century Corporation, a company Gillette founded a few years later to carry out his dream of world economic unity.

In 1895, while selling bottle stoppers in Boston, Gillette determined to change his fortunes. He went through the alphabet in search of a new product he might invent and manufacture before he found the answer staring at him in the mirror one morning. Facing the unpleasant prospect of a shave with a dull razor, he conceived the idea of a blade sharp enough on both sides to give a smooth shave, but cheap enough to toss

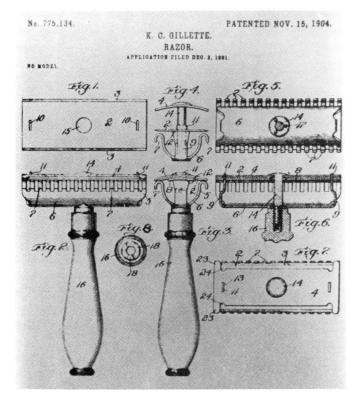

away when it became dull.

He approached metalsmiths, cutlers, and physicists at MIT for advice, and all told Gillette his idea was impractical. "If I had been a technically trained engineer," he once remarked, "I would have quit." In his case, ignorance was bliss. Nearly four years later, a craftsman in Gillette's employ finally devised a method to harden and sharpen very thin steel.

The technical challenge proved to be the least of Gillette's concerns. Potential backers all thought the idea of a disposable razor was ludicrous. Gillette convinced one investor to purchase five hundred shares in his venture for fifty cents each (he later bought them back for $62,500). In 1901, Henry Sacks, a Boston lamp manufacturer, found two other investors with enough capital to form the American Safety Razor Company. In 1904, Gillette was granted a seventeen-year patent on a double-edged disposable blade and razor.

While early sales were promising, World War I firmly established the safety razor as a habit with the male public after the government issued millions of Gillettes to American GIs. Gillette knew he was home free when, after the war, slots were installed above the basins in railroad Pullman cars for discarded blades.

Gillette retired to a California fruit farm, where he continued to conceive of plans for world economic unity. At the time of his death at age seventy-seven, his vast fortune had been reduced to about $1 million through a series of poor investments.

A box of Gillette's disposable blades.

The first Polaroid Land Camera, 1948.

The Polaroid Camera:
Inspired by an Impatient Three Year Old

While strolling down Broadway one evening in 1926, a Harvard freshman was blinded by the light of an oncoming car. It was a moment of inspiration for seventeen-year-old Edwin Herbert Land, who went on to invent the Polaroid lens and the Polaroid camera.

Born in Bridgeport, Connecticut, in 1909, Land was a precocious student who excelled in physics. After the headlight incident, he wondered if a lens to polarize light might eliminate glare. Many physicists had considered the problem, but none had succeeded in perfecting a filter that could do the job. Land left Harvard to find the solution. He moved to New York and rented a lab at Columbia University, where he worked in secrecy at night.

Having patented the synthetic lenses that are now elemental to sunglasses and camera equipment, Land returned to Harvard in 1929. He never received his degree. Three years later, he went into business with another physicist, and in 1937, he organized the Polaroid Corporation. Though Land was only twenty-eight years old, shrewd Wall Street investors such as Averell Harriman backed him and his venture. It was a wise financial move. As America readied for war, Polaroid received millions of dollars in contracts to develop military optics. By 1945, sales had multiplied from $142,000 to $17 million.

It was only the beginning. In 1943, while vacationing in Santa Fe, New Mexico, Land's three-year-old daughter Jennifer asked to see the pictures he had just taken. As he explained that it took time to develop a picture, Land was struck by the idea of instant photography. Within hours, he had worked out in his mind the process whereby an exposed print would travel through rollers, rupturing tiny pods that contained the developing chemicals.

In 1947, Land demonstrated his new invention before a group of awestruck scientists. The camera, which produced sepia-toned pictures in just sixty seconds and sold for $89.75, was introduced to the public the following year at the Jordan Marsh store in Boston. The low-budget promotion was almost as ingenious as instant photography: One department store in each major city was granted exclusive sales rights for thirty

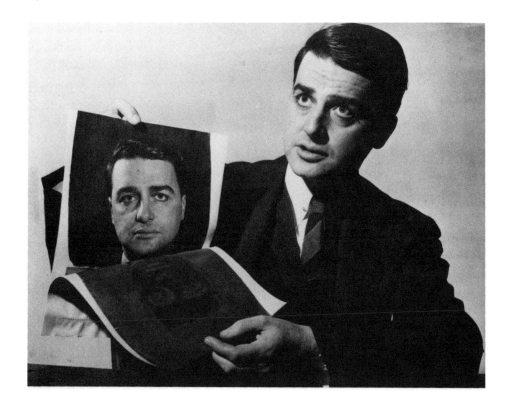

Top: *Polaroid was one of the first companies to use live television advertising, starring personalities such as Steve Allen, 1954.* Bottom: *Full color, stereoscopic movies were made possible by Polaroid's famous 3-D glasses, 1952.* Left: *Edwin H. Land demonstrating one-step photography, 1947.*

days, provided the store took charge of all advertising. It was an unqualified success.

Land could not have picked a more propitious moment. Following the end of the war, Polaroid sales had dropped to just $1.5 million with an operating loss of $2 million. But with the new camera, Polaroid climbed to second place in an industry still dominated by Eastman Kodak. Sales reached $59 million in 1958. Land never did determine whether polarized screens would reduce headlight glare; to date the auto industry has shown little interest in the project.

"No Millionaire Can Buy More Shaving Comfort"

Not many inventions have in common a restless soldier, a sprained ankle, and a moose. Then again, Lieutenant Colonel Jacob Schick, inventor of the Schick Dry Shaver, was an uncommon individual.

He was both an adventurer and a builder. At the age of sixteen, young Schick oversaw the construction of a branch railroad from his father's copper mine in Los Cerillos, New Mexico, to a coal mine down the line. By the time he joined the army in 1898, he had already spent a year prospecting in Alaska. Over the next twelve years, Schick served as an interpreter in the Philippines, as the supervisor of barracks construction projects in Michigan, and as part of the corps that dug San Francisco out from under the rubble of the 1906 earthquake. While stationed in Alaska, where he supervised the construction of a one-thousand-mile-long military telegraph, Schick also designed a new type of boat for the upper waters of the Yukon River capable of carrying fifty tons of cargo while drawing only one foot of water.

In spite of a vigorous career, Schick was plagued by ill health and bad luck throughout his life. In 1910, he retired from the army and spent the next four years working on mining explorations in the northern territories. It was during one of his sojourns in the North that Schick sprained his ankle. Forced to stay in camp for several weeks, he shot a moose for sustenance and waited for his injury to heal. With the temperature at forty degrees below zero, Schick was frustrated in his efforts to heat water to shave. As a restless soldier with time on his hands, he designed a nonelectric razor that did not require soap or water. Back in the Lower Forty-eight, he sent his plans off to potential manufacturers, but none seemed interested.

A 1934 advertisement for the Schick Dry Shaver.

26

REVOLUTIONARY NEW
SCHICK auto/home POWERSHAVE

No more stubble trouble, anywhere! At home or on the go, here's the new kind of shaver for a new kind of shave – deep down where your beard begins.

Schick's exciting new AUTO/HOME POWERSHAVE has two cords – one for home or office – one that plugs into the cigarette lighter of your car. You get fast, clean, close shaves from battery power or standard wall outlet, alike.

Now, wherever you are, you're only a cord's length away from a perfect shave.

Try it! The world's newest shaver with all the exclusive features that have made SCHICK POWERSHAVE famous. Makes a wonderful gift for Father's Day or Graduation. Most stores offer a 14-day Free Home Trial.

New Full-Contact Head. Now twice as big. Designed to hug all curves of your face—flats, rounds, hollows. Shaves you faster.

Exclusive Built-in Whisker Guides. Gently press skin down, pop whiskers out, shave you closer, deep down where your beard begins.

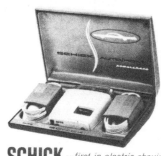

SCHICK—first in electric shaving

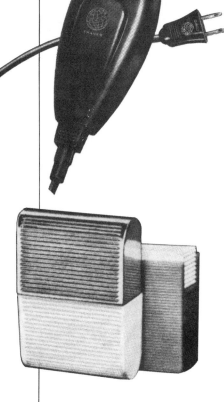

With the start of World War I, the dry shaver went on the back burner. Schick reenlisted and was stationed in London, where he transported troops to France. When he finally returned home in 1919, he began to invent. He patented a few devices for sharpening pencils. Then in 1921, Schick patented a disposable razor to compete with Gillette. None of these inventions was making the family money. Strapped for cash, his wife Florence mortgaged their home in Stamford, Connecticut, for ten thousand dollars.

While redesigning the disposable razor, Schick finally hit on the idea of an electric razor. In April of 1928, he had a design that worked on the same principle as a barber's clippers: A series of fixed slots propped up the whiskers while moving blades clipped them off. In 1931, in the heart of the Depression, the Schick Dry Shaver came to the market.

Initial sales were disappointing. "It shaved you with a loud buzz and an aroma of hot lubricating oil," one customer recalled. But with advertisements that promoted the razor as a gadget for the common man ("no millionaire can buy more shaving comfort," one ad proclaimed) and for women, the electric razor eventually took hold.

In 1935, Schick renounced his U.S. citizenship and moved to Canada, where he died eighteen months later at the age of fifty-nine.

The Search for the Perfect Pen

The ball-point pen is one of the most commonplace and simple instruments around the office. Yet it took nearly sixty years and inventors on three continents to perfect the concept patented by a Weymouth, Massachusetts, inventor back in 1888. By that time, John J. Loud had long since passed away.

Writing before the ball-point pen was inconvenient at best. The best fountain pens needed refilling often, and the worst left more ink on the writer than on the paper. So the search for the perfect writing instrument continued.

Not much is known about Loud today, except that on October 30, 1888, he received a patent for a system that delivered ink by way of a tiny, rotating ball bearing constantly bathed in fluid from a reservoir. The idea looked good on paper, sort of. Loud never figured out how to control the flow of ink to the ball bearing. The pens leaked, the paper smeared, and the ball-point remained an idea whose time had not yet come.

Enter Ladislas Biro. In 1919, Biro was an eighteen-year-old veteran of the Hungarian army in search of a moneymaker. He tried and discarded everything from medicine to painting before he and his brother Georg reinvented the ball-point pen. The Biros revealed an experimental version to a gentleman they met on the beach while on vacation. The gentleman, who proved to be Augustin Justo, president of Argentina, invited the brothers to open a factory in his country. Another twenty years passed before Ladislas took the president at his word. In 1939, he

Above: *John Jacob Loud, holding his grandson, Frederick Vickery Loud, 1910.* Right: *Loud's ball-point pen.*

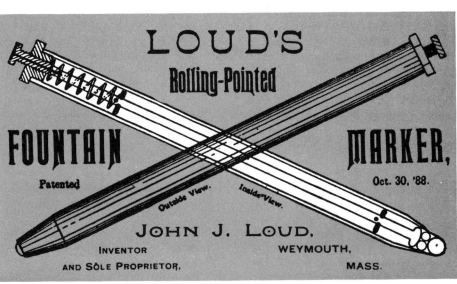

landed in Buenos Aires with ten dollars in his pocket and finally began producing ball-point pens four years later.

End of story? Not quite. Like Loud, Biro had not devised a way to control the flow of ink to the ball bearing. The pens leaked. Biro earned a profit on his invention only after he sold the North American and Caribbean marketing rights for a half-million dollars to the Sheaffer Company.

Loud's pen was now back on American soil. Sheaffer came up with a new ink compound and a spectacular advertising campaign. The ballpoint was the hit of the 1944 retail season; one department store sold one hundred thousand dollars worth of the writing instrument of the future in one day.

The pens promised more than they delivered. The new ink disappeared after exposure to sunlight, and many banks refused to honor checks signed with a ball-point. Soon, stores couldn't give them away.

Finally, in 1945, Baron Marcel Bich began to tinker with the ballpoint in a leaky shed in a Paris suburb. Within a few years, eighteen factories were producing Bic pens at the rate of seven million a day.

THE MONKEY WRENCH

With the invention of the monkey wrench by Loring Coes of Worcester, Massachusetts, in 1841, a man had only one tool to misplace rather than several.

Harvard Contributed the Brains; IBM, the Money

It could be said, without too much exaggeration, that IBM entered the computer field after the president of the corporation argued with a Harvard mathematics instructor back in August 1944.

Howard H. Aiken was the Harvard man. As a doctoral student in electrical engineering, Aiken was often frustrated by the hours he spent solving differential equations, tedious work he believed could be performed just as well by machines. The problem was that no such machine existed. So Aiken designed one, an electromechanical calculator that would link together a number of standard punch card tabulators and sorters. In 1939, he presented his plans to Thomas Watson, then the president of IBM.

In Watson, he found a favorable reception. Watson had long been interested in the application of IBM equipment to scientific purposes, not so much for the potential profit but for the favorable public relations gained from a link with a prestigious university. Having already created a research center at Columbia University, Watson readily agreed to

Above: *An early logo used by IBM.* Right: *Thomas J. Watson, Sr., 1874–1956, president of IBM.*

invest most of the five-hundred thousand dollars Aiken estimated it would take to build his computer. The navy put up the rest.

Using Aiken's plans and IBM engineers, the Automatic Sequence Controlled Calculator, or Mark I, was constructed at an IBM plant in Endicott, New York, and assembled at Harvard. The public got its first look in August of 1944, and what a wonder it was. Encased in sleek stainless steel and glass, the Mark I stood eight feet tall, two feet thick, and fifty-one feet long. Working at a rate of three calculations per second, 750,000 parts whirred and clacked as fast as twenty CPAs. One physicist said it sounded "like a roomful of ladies knitting."

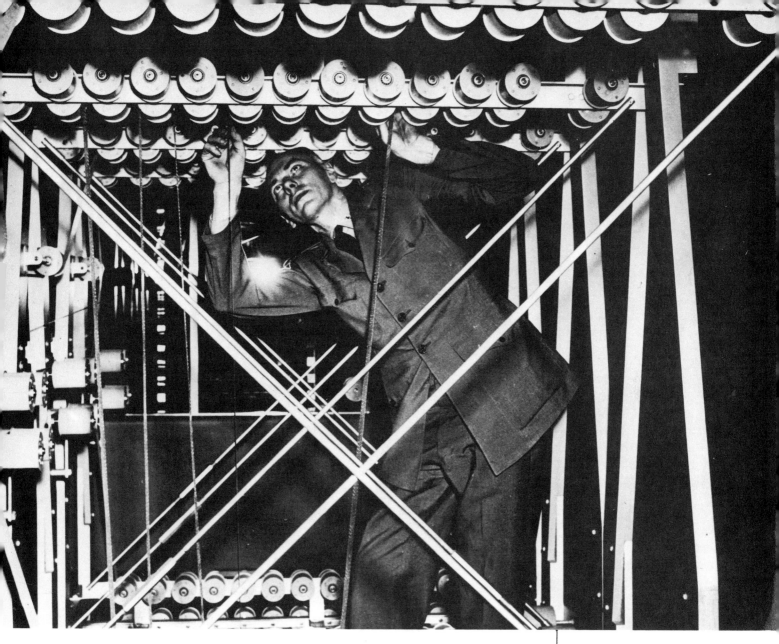

Arrogant and opinionated, Aiken barely mentioned IBM's contribution in his dedication speech. Afterwards, he and Watson had a tremendous row over the omission. "If Aiken and my father had had revolvers," Watson's son once said, "they would both have been dead." Watson was so angry, he ordered his engineers to design a better machine, and IBM was on its way to dominating the computer business.

Ironically, the computer era he ushered in soon passed by Aiken. The Mark I was built without the capacity to store programs; Aiken could see no useful purpose in a feature that is now standard on even the cheapest calculators. He once advised a couple of officials at the National Bureau of Standards to stop wasting their time and money on the effort. "There will never be enough problems, enough work for more than one or two of these computers . . ." Aiken predicted. IBM, of course, went on to sell millions of them.

Howard H. Aiken, inventor of the computer, making adjustments to the Mark I, the first computer. Compared to today's computers, this eight-foot-tall machine was very crude.

CHAPTER TWO

By Land, Sea, or Air

Those Marvelous Men & Their Rolling, Sailing, Flying Machines

Morey's Steamboat

Above: *Captain Samuel Morey.* Left: *Morey invented the steamboat, but Fulton made his fortune on it. Here is shown the* North River Steamboat, *commonly known as the* Clermont, *c. 1807.*

Hﾠistory has fostered many legends. Over the years generations of school children dutifully learned that Robert Fulton invented the steamboat. In reality, Fulton's contribution was to the world of commerce: He operated the first *profitable* steamship. A Connecticut-born Puritan named Samuel Morey ran the first paddle-driven steamboat on the Connecticut River at least thirteen years before Fulton's Folly.

Prior to the steamboat, travel between Boston and New York was an ordeal for the well-to-do and the poor alike. The overland stage bounced unmercifully on roads that were frequently impassable. Travelers were often forced to "work their passage" by pushing the coach out of the mud. The two-hundred mile trip often consumed a week. The water route, on the other hand, was more comfortable; but since sailing vessels were the exclusive mode of travel, the length of a voyage was entirely dependent upon the wind. And the wind was one thing the stern Puritans could not regulate.

Enter Captain Samuel Morey, a lumber merchant from Orford, New Hampshire, who decided to defy both God and Nature to find a means of locomotion without wind.

Morey first became interested in steam power around 1790, when he harnessed the steam from a kettle to turn the spit in his fireplace. He applied the same logic to his boat, a small vessel with a paddle wheel attached to the bow which pulled the boat along. Years later, he would discover that the boat operated more efficiently with the paddle wheel in the stern.

One Sunday morning in 1793, Morey launched the *Aunt Sally* while the rest of the town was at church, apparently so his neighbors could not laugh at him if he failed. The boat was just large enough to contain Morey, rude machinery connected with a steam boiler, and a handful of wood for the fire. Crossing the river to Fairlee, Vermont, Morey achieved the exhilarating speed of five miles an hour.

For the next three summers, Morey operated steamboats on the rivers of New York. Then in 1795 or '96, a family illness caused Morey to leave the city. Quite naturally, he went by steamboat, across Long Island Sound and up the Connecticut to Hartford, at that time the longest single voyage under steam.

Morey never received the credit due for his achievement. Though he was plagued by financial setbacks, he once turned down seven thousand dollars and the promise of more money if he could develop a boat capable of eight miles an hour. Discouraged by Fulton's success, he spent the last years of his life in Fairlee, where he operated a boat on a small lake that now bears his name. In a gesture of frustration, Morey sank his boat in the middle of the lake. According to legend, the boat can be heard chugging about in circles on misty nights.

Louis Downing

J. Stephen Abbott

The Coach That Won the Prairie

On September 16, 1857, a stagecoach carrying mail and papers left San Francisco for St. Louis. It was an historic occasion nearly a year in preparation, the first trip over the new mail route linking east with west. Rotating a team of six horses every twelve to fifteen miles, the coach traveled one hundred miles a day, sometimes more, and arrived in St. Louis well ahead of the twenty-five-day schedule. Considering the pounding it had just taken, the Concord coach was in remarkable condition, just as its makers back in New Hampshire had predicted all along. If Colt made the gun that won the West, then Abbott, Downing made the coach that conquered the prairie.

The Concord coach was the creation of Louis Downing. When he hung out his shingle in 1813 at the age of twenty-one, Downing had sixty dollars in his pocket, a few tools, and an apprenticeship served in his father's shop. A dozen years later, he was joined by J. Stephen Abbott, a coach maker from Salem, and John Borgum, an English landscape painter.

Together they designed a new coach for long-distance travel. The roof top was flat to accommodate luggage and adventuresome pas-

The famous Concord Coach,
loaded with passengers.

sengers; the wheels and body were constructed from the best seasoned
woods available; and the coach was suspended on braces of cowhide for
a relatively smooth ride, given the conditions of the roads.

By 1868, when thirty Concord coaches valued at forty-five thousand dollars were loaded onto a single train and shipped to Salt Lake
City for use over the Sierra Nevada Mountains, they were not only the
stagecoach of choice for crossing the country, but also the coach pre-
ferred by fine hotels, such as the Astor in New York, the Tremont in Boston, and the Palmer House in Chicago. A Concord coach even ascended
Mt. Washington.

Eventually, the stagecoach fell out of popularity in favor of the locomotive and the steam buggy. Abbott, Downing finally closed the doors
on its six-acre facility just after the turn of the century. In all, more than
three thousand stagecoaches, sold for about $850 a piece, had been
shipped around the world.

Out of the Maine Woods

It came from the Maine woods with a surge of flying sparks: a wood-
burning steam engine mounted on crawling tracks, dragging as much
timber in its wake as a team of one hundred horses. Within thirty years,
the tractor invented by Alvin Orlando Lombard would be replaced by
other equipment, but the means of locomotion by steel tracks, or lags,
would be adapted to the army tank and the bulldozer.

Born in 1856 on a small farm in Springfield, Maine, Lombard first
directed his creative energies to improving his father's blacksmith shop
and sawmill. By 1899, Lombard's devices were running paper mills and
the iron foundries at the Waterville Iron Works. An automatic control for

Photographs of the early log hauler. Lombard is seen standing just to the right of the cab in the top picture.

water wheels and turbines was still in use on hydroelectric plants as recently as the 1960s.

His most important device was the tractor tread. After a chance conversation one afternoon, Lombard decided to build a log hauler and emancipate the horse from the killing hauls over tote roads. Lombard went straight home and began to work without supper. Within two days, he had a wooden model sitting on a desk at the iron works.

Building the log hauler was another story. Steam was the logical choice of power, but in some way a tractive mechanism had to be devised that would not only grip the ground but also adjust itself to any irregularities. It would have to lay its own wide rails. Lombard experimented until he recalled a horse-driven treadmill he had seen as a boy. The first Lombard hauler, the "Mary Ann," was built for the Brown Company in time for the 1900-1901 logging season.

At first, the horse was not entirely eliminated. Lombard's plans called for a team to be hitched in front of the engine to do the steering. For the horses it must have seemed as though they had gone from the pan into the fire. Now there was a pushing, steam-breathing devil tied to their tails. When horses proved reluctant navigators, Lombard stationed a man in front, who bent over a wheel and wrestled to keep a pair of steering sled runners in the proper ruts while sparks from the smokestack landed on his mackinaw.

Flames, sparks, and hot metal were minor inconveniences for the steerer. There were no brakes on the log hauler, and nearly every wooded road had a downgrade that made steerers pray for their survival.

Solving the technical problems were the least of Lombard's woes. On May 21, 1901, he was awarded a patent for the iron monster. By that time, companies as far away as California were infringing on his patent rights. Then came the gasoline engines, and the iron monster was dead in its tracks. The last operation for Lombard's log haulers was in 1928 at a place called Cooper Brook, Maine.

When Yankees Ruled the Roads

Detroit receives all the credit, but the automobile industry was born in New England, and for a brief time Yankees ruled the roads. In 1866, Henry Alonzo House patented the "Horseless Carriage" in Bridgeport, Connecticut; George Brayton of Boston patented the two-stroke internal combustion engine in 1872; and the Duryea Motor Wagon Company of Springfield, Massachusetts, produced the first commercial automobiles in 1895.

But the real struggle for the American auto industry did not take place on the show-room floors but in the courts. The litigants were Henry Ford and a patent attorney named George Baldwin Selden. Had the courts ruled differently, Hartford, Connecticut, might be the center of the auto industry today.

Along with a successful law practice in Rochester, New York, Selden had a penchant for invention. In 1876, he visited the Centennial Exhibition in Philadelphia where he viewed the new stationary engine designed by George Brayton. Back home, Selden worked out on paper a way to install a lighter version of the Brayton engine in a "road wagon" and transmit power to the front wheels by means of a clutch and gearshift; in other words, he had invented the car. In 1879, Selden submitted

George Baldwin Selden and one of his sons, posing in front of the car built in Rochester in 1905 to forestall a patent challenge from Henry Ford. Note the date tacked onto the side of the cab.

an application to the Patent Office.

While Selden possessed neither the mechanical skill nor the money to manufacture his car, he did have a keen sense of the law. If he continued to file additional claims, he could delay the issuance of a patent until someone else tried to go into the automobile business. Then, they would have to deal with Selden. Since no one was attempting to build automobiles, the attorney kept his application open until November 5, 1895, just a few weeks before the first official auto race was won in Chicago by a Duryea Wagon.

That same year, Colonel Albert Pope, an influential bicycle manufacturer from Hartford, formed a company to build electric taxicabs. The Electric Vehicle Company paid Selden ten thousand dollars plus the promise of future royalties for the rights to his patent. The taxis were a failure, but after several court cases, Pope formed the Association of Licensed Automobile Manufacturers in 1903. Anyone who wanted to manufacture automobiles would have to pay the association a royalty of 1.25 percent of the retail price of each car. The lion's share went to Electric Vehicle and Selden.

Only one manufacturer held out: Henry Ford. As Ford's automobiles began to sell, the association filed suit and warned the public that anyone purchasing a Ford was in for a battle. Ford and his leading dealers countered with the offer of a surety bond with each vehicle.

The matter ended up in the courts. Selden wanted to forestall any

Taken in New York City in 1907, this photograph shows a demonstration run of Selden's machine. The mechanic jogging next to the car was there to restart the balky engine each time it stalled, which was quite frequently. His name: Cranky Louis.

attempt by Ford to claim that the car described in his patent would not have worked. So thirty years after filing the original application, the first two Selden cars were manufactured. One was built in Rochester, the other in the Electric Vehicle shops in Hartford.

Both cars moved under their own power, but barely. That was enough for the court: The judge ruled the patent was valid, and Henry Ford was an infringer. Two years later, the decision was reversed on appeal, and the association called it quits. Meanwhile, Electric Vehicle had failed in the panic of 1907.

Though the auto industry ultimately left New England, Selden's biographer estimated that he earned two hundred thousand dollars from royalties. Not bad, wrote the biographer, "for a patent finally adjudged as completely devoid of commercial value." In 1963 the Ford-Selden fight was in the news again when the Stevens Institute of Technology at Hoboken, New Jersey, presented the Selden-Rochester car to the Henry Ford Museum at Dearborn, Michigan. The other car is on exhibit at the museum of the Connecticut State Library in Hartford.

Above left: *Henry Ford and the "quadricycle,"* c. 1896.

The Stanley Steamer

Francis Edgar Stanley, the identical twin of Freelan Oscar Stanley, was an athletic fellow who wanted his wife to ride the bicycle with him. But Mrs. Stanley, who weighed two hundred pounds, was not very agile. She tried once, fell off, and gave it up, but F. E. promised to build something they could ride together. The Stanley Steamer automobile was born.

From their boyhood days in Kingfield, Maine, F. E. and F. O. had always been mechanically inclined. By 1897, the twins had patented the first machine for coating dry photographic plates and operated a thriving factory in Newton, Massachusetts. That summer at a local fair, they watched as a French inventor demonstrated his steam-driven car. A quarter of the way around the track, the car stalled and would not start.

After the fair, F. E. began to tinker with variations of the Frenchman's design. In 1898, the brothers formed the Stanley Motor Carriage Company. With only a few moving parts, "The Flying Teapot" was easy to run and reached the blistering speed of thirty-five miles an hour with one drawback: Every ten miles or so the boiler had to be refilled with

The Stanley twins in their steam-driven car, c. 1897.

water. In 1899, F. O. made history when he and his wife drove to the top of Mt. Washington in two hours and ten minutes. He could have done it faster, he said afterwards, if he hadn't had to stop all the time for water. Three years later, an improved Steamer made the mountain climb in twenty-seven minutes.

With all the favorable publicity, Stanley Steamers sold like lemonade on a summer day. The brothers pocketed a fast $250,000 on the sale of the company and returned full time to the plate business. But they had been bitten by the automobile bug. In 1905, George Eastman, the founder of Kodak, obtained the Stanleys' rights to their plate process, and the brothers converted their Newton factory into an automobile plant. They were back in the car business.

Having already scaled the heights of Mt. Washington, the twins hired driver Fred Marriott to race their cars. In January of 1906, Marriott drove "The Rocket" to a land-speed record of 127.659 miles an hour at Ormond Beach, Florida. He was the first human to travel faster than 2 miles a minute. The following year, Marriott was traveling at nearly 200 miles an hour when he hit a bump and flew one hundred feet in the air before crash landing. Marriott survived.

F. E. Stanley was not so lucky. One day in 1918, he was approaching the top of a hill in a Stanley Steamer when he suddenly noticed the road ahead was blocked by a couple of wagons. Stanley turned the wheel of his car and was killed when he crashed into a woodpile and plunged down an embankment.

The accident was also the end of the Stanley Steamer. F. O., recuperating from tuberculosis in Colorado, was in his sixties. With World War I rumbling on another continent, car production was mothballed, and steam engines were shipped to Europe, where they were used to pump water out of trenches. After the war, Ford's gasoline Tin Lizzies dominated the market, and the Stanley Company was eventually taken over by the banks. Late in his life, F. O. returned to Newton, where he and a nephew built violins in a shop near his home.

The Electric Car Meets Edison

In 1898, S. R. Bailey and his son Edwin were the best carriage makers in the country. Bailey and Company, located in Amesbury, Massachusetts, was riding high thanks to the glass windshield, an innovation S. R. had come up with to distinguish their craft from the rest of the trade.

All the same, the father and son team were apprehensive about the future of the horse and buggy. When he joined the army that year, young Ed heard a great deal of talk about the motor car, recently brought to a practical state in Europe. Fascinated, the young colonel wrote his father: "The motor car is the future vehicle . . . . [W]e should do well to look into the possibility of doing something with it."

When Colonel Bailey arrived home, his father escorted him into the factory and showed off the Bailey Company's latest experiment: a beautiful carriage fitted with an electric motor. It was perfect except for one minor detail: The batteries were so heavy, the car would not move.

Though the Baileys remained undaunted, nearly a decade passed before they refined the electric car. The first practical model went on exhibit in 1908. Even then, they were limited to a fifty-mile or so range between charges.

The breakthrough came about five years later when Thomas Edison perfected an improved storage battery. Edison wanted to test his battery under the roughest conditions possible, and so he chose the best

Above: *"The ideal ladies' car"* boasted an ad for Bailey's electric car. *"Its ease of control, safety appliances, wide range on one charge of battery, together with its simple and rugged construction and comfortable riding qualities make it the ideal car for a lady to use when calling, shopping, or pleasure driving."*
Right: *Thomas Edison is standing by one of Bailey's test cars at the end of an endurance run. The driver is George Langdon and the passenger is Frank McGinnis.*

carriage made at the time. The Bailey test cars were driven hundreds of miles over the most miserable roads imaginable. A Bailey car climbed Ft. George Hill twenty-one times on one battery charge and made a one-thousand-mile endurance run without incident. Like the Stanley Steamer, it even climbed Mt. Washington.

Edison's batteries withstood the rigors of his tests, and by extension, so did the Baileys' car. With the famous inventor's endorsement, they went all out to promote their vehicles. A Bailey electric with Edison batteries could travel more than one hundred miles without recharging, at twenty-two miles per hour. To demonstrate their reliability, Colonel Bailey drove one of the cars from Boston to Chicago in miserable weather over roads only slightly better than those used by Hannibal to cross the Alps. The car performed beautifully; it was rugged, efficient, and masterfully crafted.

Unfortunately, no one bought them. The death blow to the electric car was the self-starter, another electrical device. When the most fragile woman on the block could march out in zero-degree weather and, by pushing a button, turn over an engine that would have required a gorilla to crank, one of the electric's major selling points evaporated. Production ceased in 1915.

The Very First Flying Machine

In December of 1903, Orville and Wilbur Wright made history near Kitty Hawk, North Carolina, when their flying machine "raised itself by its own power into the air in free flight." The flight lasted twelve seconds and, in the view of most historians, ushered in the age of "true flight."

That same view is not held in Bridgeport, Connecticut. According to a full-page article published August 17, 1901, in the *Bridgeport Sunday*

Above: *Gustave Alvin Whitehead (c. 1901) with one of the first aircraft engines made in this country. It's a two-cylinder, two-cycle, air-cooled gasoline engine.* Below: The Bridgeport Sunday Herald *reported that Whitehead flew his "No. 21" aircraft on August 19, 1901, at a maximum height of about fifty feet for about a half mile.*

Herald, Gustave Alvin Whitehead, a local Bavarian immigrant, was the first in flight. The reporter claimed to have witnessed the event four days earlier, when Whitehead took off from Tunxis Hill, in nearby Fairfield, Connecticut, and flew under power for nearly half a mile at a maximum height of about fifty feet. On January 17, 1902, Whitehead is supposed to have flown his craft for seven miles, a trip the inventor dubbed unsuccessful because it did not incorporate a vertical takeoff and landing.

Whitehead continued his experiments with flight for years. He built triplanes, biplanes, and even an early version of the helicopter with sixty blades. The flights of Gustave Whitehead, however, have never been fully credited because it was thought no photo existed (but two were uncovered in 1982). In a letter published in the April 1902 issue of the *American Inventor,* Whitehead did ask the editor to be present to photograph his continued successful flights. The editor never showed, and the inventor did not pursue his claim; he believed a true flight was one in which an airplane would rise vertically into the air like a bird and fly. Whitehead was never satisfied that any of his flights were successful. When World War I came along, his German nationality effectively stopped any possible recognition of his work. Whitehead died a pauper on October 10, 1927.

The controversy over Whitehead's possible achievement has raged since 1937, when Stella Randolph of Garrett Park, Maryland, published her book, *The Lost Flights of Gustave Whitehead.* Randolph was roundly condemned by aviation historians as "unreliable and unqualified."

An artist's rendering
of Whitehead's
flying machine.

Still, a dedicated bunch from the 9315th Air Force Reserve Squadron of Stratford is bent on establishing Whitehead's legitimacy. As William J. O'Dwyer, the driving force behind the group, wrote in *Yankee,* "In every nation around the globe, men have been handed the death penalty for a crime, based upon the eyewitness account of a single individual. If 'flying' had been a crime punishable by death in 1901, then poor Gus Whitehead would have gone to the gallows." Undaunted, the squadron reconstructed a model of Whitehead's 1901 powered monoplane and flew it in December 1968, proving Whitehead's flights were no fluke.

But, at this writing in 1988, the opinion of the Smithsonian Institution has not changed from that expressed by Paul Garber, assistant director for aeronautics, in a letter to *Yankee* dated August 28, 1968. "Whitehead certainly has a place in history but not as the first person to achieve free flight in a heavier-than-air craft under power and control."

A Design That Shouldn't Work

In 1909, Igor Ivanovitch Sikorsky, a twenty year old from Kiev, Russia, conducted his first experiments with a helicopter. While it did not fly, Sikorsky was optimistic. "It seemed to be trying to get into the air," he said. Twenty years later in Stratford, Connecticut, the first modern helicopter took off with the Russian at the controls.

The son of a renowned doctor and professor, Sikorsky had been inspired by the stories his mother first read to him about Leonardo da Vinci's helicopter designs. In 1908, when news of the Wright brothers finally reached Kiev, Sikorsky was overwhelmed with a desire to learn to fly. He immediately went to Paris and bought a twenty-five-horsepower engine. He was going to build machines for flight.

He began with a twin-rotor helicopter. Though it did not fly, Sikorsky was more fortunate building fixed-wing aircraft. Piloting his sixth design, he set a world speed record of seventy miles an hour. On May 13, 1913, he defied conventional wisdom and flew the first multi-engined airplane with an enclosed cabin. "The Grand" had four 100-horsepower

Igor Sikorsky demonstrating America's first "windmill" plane, the helicopter, 1939.

engines, a washroom, living room, and observation deck. The Russian Army bought seventy-five of his planes and used them to bomb Germany during World War I. By the time he was thirty, Sikorsky had amassed a fortune of more than five hundred thousand dollars.

He fled the Russian Revolution for New York, where he taught mathematics to other immigrants. By 1923, however, he was back in the aircraft business. Sikorsky Aero Engineering Corporation almost went broke when its first airplane crashed. But soon, Sikorsky was building Pan American Airline's flying boat, the plane that ushered in the era of transoceanic passenger service. Just before the stock market debacle of 1929, United Aircraft bought his company.

Ten years later, Sikorsky resumed his experiments on the helicopter. Other designers at the time were trying to build helicopters with two rotors. Since he had already traveled that path, Sikorsky built a prototype with a single rotor. On September 14, 1939, wearing his blue business suit and a fedora with the brim turned up on end, Sikorsky flew the VS-300.

It was a herky-jerky affair. He had figured out how to get it in the air but not how to control the mechanical insect. For the next two years, he tinkered on his "bumblebee" behind the factory in Stratford, Connecticut, always dressed in his trademark blue suit and fedora. At the same time, he was also learning how to fly the craft. "We built the first helicopter by what we hoped was intelligent guess," he would later comment in his fractured English. In May of 1942, after nineteen major alterations, Sikorsky delivered the first XR–4 helicopter to the air force at Wright Field, Ohio.

Up to the end of his life, Sikorsky acknowledged that by design the helicopter should not fly. "The bumblebee doesn't know this," he would add, "so he goes ahead and flies away." The fedora hat he favored during his test flights is still kept at his old office at Sikorsky Aircraft.

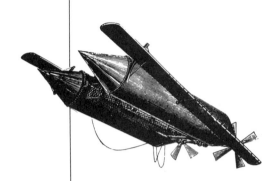

Up, Up, & Away

Like another American legend, this story begins with a cherry tree. Unlike the fantasy of George Washington and his hatchet, this story is true.

On October 19, 1899, on a farm outside Worcester, Massachusetts,

Robert Goddard with his mother on the grounds of Maple Hill, Worcester, Massachusetts, where he was first inspired with the idea of interplanetary flight.

Above: *Dr. Robert Goddard standing beside the first liquid-fueled rocket, 1926.* Right: *At the scene of a misfired rocket, 1929. Goddard (second from left) was not discouraged, but his assistant, Percy Roope (right), was.*

a young man named Robert Hutchings Goddard climbed a cherry tree to do some pruning for his grandmother, who owned the farm. He had turned seventeen years old two weeks before, and in his leafy reverie Goddard was suddenly struck by "how wonderful it would be to make some device which had even the possibility of ascending to Mars. . . . . " He imagined a sort of whirligig propelled by centrifugal force — an idea his cousin, who went to Harvard, told him would never work.

Goddard, whose father called him "the angel shooter," became obsessed with the idea of interplanetary flight. By 1909, he had outlined half a dozen methods of space propulsion, all of them wildly imaginative in his day, all of them either in use or under consideration in ours. In one of his private notebooks, there is a detailed description of a winged "car" driven by "explosive jets of liquid hydrogen and liquid oxygen," steered by "side-jets" — in other words, a space shuttle. The press dubbed him "The Moon Man."

The drawings in his notebooks became real on March 16, 1926. Goddard was then chairman of the physics department at Clark University in Worcester. Accompanied by his wife and two assistants, he

Left: *Dr. Goddard (left) at work in his laboratory with a rocket that was the precise forerunner of today's launch vehicles.*
Below: *Goddard supervising adjustments to a rocket with turbopumps in its launching tower near Roswell, New Mexico, 1940. The sheath and nose cone had not yet been installed.*

launched the first liquid-fueled rocket from his Aunt Effie's farm. One of the assistants ignited the engine by means of an ordinary blowtorch on the end of a long rod, and the rocket rose just 41 feet before crashing into Aunt Effie's cabbage patch, 184 feet away. The whole flight lasted 2.5 seconds. Goddard was delighted.

The milestone was not appreciated, even by those in attendance. Henry Sachs, one of the assistants, observed that he could have thrown a baseball farther. In July of 1929, a new rocket rose to about ninety feet and then exploded after hitting the ground sixty yards away. Soon the police arrived on the scene, accompanied by reporters. The headline in the *Boston Globe* read: "Moon Rocket Man's Test Alarms Whole Countryside." The state fire marshal ordered Goddard to cease testing his machines in the Commonwealth.

Rocket research finally received a boost the following November. Charles Lindbergh, having read news accounts of the tests, eventually persuaded financier Daniel Guggenheim to grant Goddard one hundred thousand dollars for four years of work. Goddard left his teaching duties and moved to Roswell, New Mexico, where he continued his research in the privacy of the desert. At the time of his death in August of 1945, Goddard had received two hundred patents for rocketry.

In 1969, the day after *Apollo 11* left earth orbit for the moon, a *New York Times* editorial recalled that the paper had once sneered at Goddard's contention that rockets could operate in outer space. They apologized for the error.

CHAPTER THREE

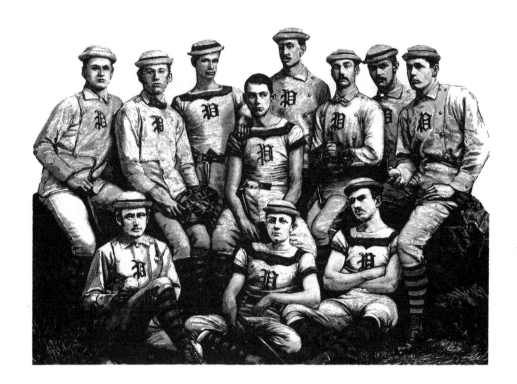

For Fun & Profit

The Games People Play

The Iceman Cometh

Forty years takes us back to the dawn of history as far as the New England ski industry is concerned. Of course there were ski slopes in the thirties, but they were rather experimental in nature and were run as winter adjuncts to the owners' "real" occupations.

It wasn't until after World War II that a few people began to think of skiing as having any business potential. One of these pioneers was Walt Schoenknecht, an avid skier from the East Haven Ski Club and a Marine Corps veteran. When he got out of the service, Walt was determined to make a living from the sport he loved. After he acquired rights to cut ski trails on Connecticut's third-highest peak, he began hacking away at the trees early in 1947.

The first season still stands as the snowiest in Mohawk's four-decade history. The second year had plentiful natural snowfall, too. The ski area prospered, and within a couple of years, Walt had ten rope tows hauling as many as thirty-five hundred skiers a day up Mohawk Mountain. Now it would be nice to be able to report that the Schoenknechts and their mountain lived happily, and without setbacks, forever after. But in a business as fickle as the ski industry, that was not to be.

Everyone who was involved in skiing forty years ago still remembers the winter of 1949–50 as the winter it didn't snow. Anxiously, Mohawk skiers watched for December snow clouds, but none came. In January the earth was cold and barren, and so was the sky. Nary a flake fell on Litchfield County.

Now Walt Schoenknecht is not a man to let a lack of snow be an obstacle to running his ski area. He had been to nearby Salisbury, where an old ski jump was regularly blanketed with snow made from finely crushed ice. If this would work on a ski jump, Walt reasoned, it ought to work on the mountain as well.

If there was ever a time when ice was available for such an endeavor, it was in those early postwar years. People had recently switched from ice boxes to refrigerators, and the old ice houses hadn't folded yet.

Walt located a behemoth ice crusher and set it up at the foot of Mohawk Mountain early during the last week of January 1950. He hired local farmers and their four-wheel-drive trucks. He bought five hundred tons of block ice from the Economy Ice Company in Torrington, the nearest major city to Mohawk. At first, seventeen trucks shuttled back and forth between Torrington and the mountain, hauling ice twenty-four hours a day. But soon the crew on the mountain grew, and more trucks had to be added, until there were nearly thirty.

Cindy Ellis, Frank Ellis, and Walt Schoenknecht watching the ice crusher in action, 1950.

The men formed a human chain from the trucks to the hungry maw of the pulverizer, passing huge chunks of ice from hand to hand and dropping them into the hopper. Every time a one-hundred-pound block was plopped into the machine, its fast-churning blades would buzz, and much like a modern food processor instantly chopping a carrot, the monster would spit a stream of fine powder snow onto the slope.

Wednesday became Thursday, and Thursday's sun began to set. The crews kept growing, because everyone wanted to be in on the act. The ribbon of white continued creeping up the mountain. After a time, the Torrington ice houses, emptied of their stocks, were making ice as fast as they could. Before Walt was through, he would clean out the ice houses as far away as New Milford and Waterbury.

The only moment of panic occurred in the wee hours of Friday night, when the last of the herculean pre-weekend snowmaking efforts were being made. One of the weary workers accidentally dropped a pair of heavy ice tongs into the whirring blades of the pulverizer. To a man, the crew froze in place as the most horrible groaning sounds emanated from the innards of the pulverizer. The slopes were three-quarters covered. It would be terrible if the machine conked out then.

"The crazy thing," recalls Walt Schoenknecht, "is that the machine never stopped. It made the darnedest sounds, crashing sounds, thrashing sounds. But it completely cut up the tongs and threw them out with the snow. The only thing that happened was that the knives got nicked, so the pulverizer started making corn snow instead of powder, but it was just as good to ski on."

The Ski Tow Popularized Skiing

Like Marcus Urann and the cranberry and Ford with his automobile, Bunny Bertram was a populist — he helped bring skiing in America to the masses with his cheap, reliable rope tow.

In 1933, Bertram, the former captain of the Dartmouth ski team, took a ride on Foster's Folly, a rope tow on "The Big Hill" at Shawbridge,

Bunny Bertram

The crowds lined up to try out America's first rope tow, installed in Woodstock, Vermont, at the White Cupboard Hill. The tow was installed in 1934.

Quebec — without question the first rope tow in the free world. Back in Woodstock, Vermont, Bertram and Clint Gilbert strung a rope up Gilbert's Hill at the White Cupboard Inn. The flywheel of a Ford tractor powered the lift, which premiered in February 1934. At normal speeds, it took about one minute to reach the top of the hill. Bertram, however, often amused himself by running the rope at a breakneck speed of twenty-five miles per hour, sending unwary skiers into orbit at the end of the lift. The following year, the Bertram/Gilbert tow was installed at the Suicide Six Ski Area in Woodstock.

One of the skiers during that first year in operation was Theodore C. Cooke, an engineer from New Hampshire who was convinced that anything Bertram could do, he could do better. In the fall of 1934, Cooke began construction on a two-stage, three-thousand-foot tow at Gunstock Mountain, New Hampshire. The longest rope tow in the free world opened the following year. Cooke's tow was in operation until 1939, when it was sold to the Commonwealth Country Club in Boston.

Films of those early lifts have been preserved at the New England Ski Museum at Cannon Mountain, in Franconia Notch, New Hampshire.

Baseball's Great Equalizer

Along with less polite terms, the curve ball has been called baseball's great equalizer.

"If it hadn't been for the curve," said Martin Quigley, author of *The Crooked Pitch,* "baseball would be a game for muscular apes. It's the reason a man who hits three out of ten for his career is an automatic hall of famer."

Arthur "Candy" Cummings, of Ware, Massachusetts, is considered the originator of the crooked pitch. Born on October 17, 1848, his nickname was attributed to a sweet pitching style and slight stature. "God never gave him any size," commented one of his managers, "but he's the candy." When Candy Cummings entered organized ball in 1866, with the Hercules of Fulton, New York, he stood just five feet nine inches tall and weighed only 120 pounds.

He thought up the curve ball in 1862 as a boy of fourteen. He tossed a clam shell into the sea and noted its curve. Two years later, he duplicated the effect by holding a baseball in a "death grip" and twisting his wrist on release of an underhand pitch. By the 1866-67 season, when Cummings was playing for the Brooklyn Excelsiors, he had developed a

Arthur Cummings

dependable curve which he kept under wraps. "I was jealous of it," he said, "and did not want anyone to crib it."

He finally unveiled the curve in 1867 against Harvard. The idea that a pitch could swerve just before it reached the batter attracted fascination and derision. Some fans thought it the work of the devil. Harvard physics students and teachers knew that it was impossible and came to the game to jeer Cummings. In his words, he "curve-balled them to death." Cummings went on to play eleven more years in the major leagues, ending his career in 1878 with Forest City of Cleveland. He is believed to be the first pitcher to throw and win a double-header, against the Cincinnati Red Legs.

Whether or not the ball actually curves has been a matter of debate ever since 1867. After photographic experiments, both *Life* and *Look* concluded the curve is an optical illusion. Ernest Lowry, a passionate Canadian, unsuccessfully argued his entire adult life that the curve ball is "a connivance of baseball profiteers and the press." In 1952, Lowry asked his government to extradite baseball officials to stand trial for fraud. On the other hand, Igor Sikorsky, inventor of the helicopter, devised a formula to calculate the trajectory of the pitch.

Former Phillies manager Eddie Sawyer has the last word on the subject: "I am not positive whether a ball curves or not. But if this pitch

Top: *The Brooklyn Excelsiors, c. 1860. Cummings is standing third from the left.* Bottom: *The path of a curve ball in a continuous curve from the time the ball leaves the pitcher's hand.*

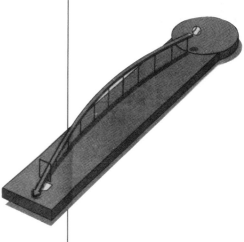

does not curve, it would be well to notify a lot of players who quit the game they loved because of this pitch, and who can now be reached at numerous gas stations, river docks, and mental institutions."

Left: Billy McGunnigle played for the Buffalo Bisons. This photo was probably taken in 1878, when the Bisons belonged to the International Association, which was comprised of minor leagues. Right: This ad for Spalding equipment appeared in 1888.

The First "Tools of Ignorance"

Prior to the "tools of ignorance," as Washington Senators catcher Muddy Ruel referred to catcher's equipment, taking up the position behind home plate required the nerve of a test pilot. This was especially true after 1890 when overhand pitching was introduced to the game, and the pitcher's mound was moved back from fifty feet to sixty feet six inches. Presumably, injuries to catchers increased in direct proportion to

the increase in velocity; while a team might carry only one or two pitchers, a whole platoon of catchers was required to complete a game.

William "Gunner" McGunnigle, a Fall River, Massachusetts, receiver is credited with wearing the pair of bricklayer's gloves that spawned the invention of the catcher's mitt in a game against Harvard in 1875. After the game, James Tyng, an outfielder and substitute catcher for Harvard, bought a pair of mason's mitts and inserted thin lead sheets into the palms for the first modified catching glove.

By 1891, heavily padded gloves specifically for catchers were being marketed by several sporting goods companies, including the Spalding Company of Chicopee, Massachusetts. An 1890s advertisement for Spalding's "Trade Marked Catcher's Gloves" lists four different models ranging in price from two to five dollars. "No player subject to sore hands should be without a pair," the ad urged.

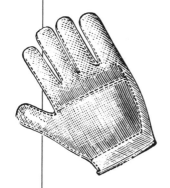

The modern "break" glove manufactured by Spalding is capable of fielding pitches of more than ninety miles an hour and costs more than ten times the original.

The catcher's mask, incidentally, was first used by Winthrop Thayer, who played for Harvard, in a game against Live Oaks on April 12, 1877. Winthrop probably devised the mask he used.

Straighten Up & Fly Right

Just as Kleenex has become the generic term for a facial tissue, Wiffle Ball is used by the uninformed to cover any plastic substitute for a baseball. However, the only true Wiffle Ball is covered under patent #2,776,139 and has eight oblong holes in one half. It is manufactured in Shelton, Connecticut.

David Mullany, Sr., a salesman for an auto polish firm, invented the ball after watching his son David Mullany, Jr., and his friend "Rubber John" Bellus trying to master the art of the curve ball. A former semipro pitcher, Mullany Sr. understood the damage a curve ball can inflict on a young arm and set out to design a lightweight ball that would curve by itself. On a summer day in 1953, he obtained a dozen plastic balls used to hold perfume from the nearby Coty factory and cut holes in them with a razor blade. His son and Rubber John tested the various designs in the backyard, shouting "I whiffed you!" whenever the batter went down swinging at the gyrating sphere. A version with eight oblong holes in one half worked best.

The Wiffle Ball might have remained just a backyard prototype

David Mullany, Jr., and David Mullany, Sr.

if it had not been for a stroke of bad luck: The auto polish company closed. Out of work, Mullany Sr. mortgaged his house and began marketing Wiffle Balls. It took two years before a manufacturer's rep named Saul Mondschein persuaded a few retailers to carry the ball, but since then the game has caught on in all fifty states, Europe, and even Guam, without the benefit of advertising. "Wiffle balls sell themselves," David Mullany, Jr., has claimed. He now runs the factory.

One fan called the Wiffle Ball "the most unaerodynamic projectile ever conceived: It will dip, rise, twist, wiggle, and do a fair rendition of Chuck Berry's duck strut. . . . [I]t will do about anything but straighten up and fly right."

James Naismith

The One True American Sport

Basketball is considered the one truly American sport. While baseball evolved from cricket and rounders, football from soccer and rugby, basketball has no antecedent in the foreign sports world.

The officially accepted story of basketball's origins goes something like this: In 1891, James Naismith, a former seminary student from Canada and a professor at the International YMCA College in Springfield, Massachusetts, developed a sport that could be played indoors, at night, in winter. He nailed two peach baskets to the opposite walls of a gym and published the rules in the school paper, *The Triangle,* on January 15, 1892. The first game took place on January 20, 1892. Teams were made up of nine players each, and the game was played over three periods of twenty minutes each with a soccer ball. Players were not allowed to run with the ball; scoring took place by passing to teammates who worked for position. Dribbling, then, was invented when players realized they could pass to themselves by bouncing the ball off the floor. In 1894, the soccer ball was replaced by the modern-size basketball. The backboard was invented to stop partisan fans from interfering with the play.

In just four years, basketball spread across the country. It was a game equally popular with men and women. Naismith met his wife, Maude Sherman, while teaching basketball to the schoolmarms from Buckingham Grade School in Springfield. The first intercollegiate game was played between the University of Chicago and University of Iowa on January 16, 1896. Chicago won 15-12. In 1904, basketball was played in the St. Louis Olympic Games.

That said, there is at least one Holyoke, Massachusetts, woman who disputes Naismith's claim to fame. Ms. Clara Gabler remembers that her

Top: *James Naismith demonstrating the principles of basketball to an aspiring player.* Left: *A basketball game played in 1892. A real basket was used for equipment. Notice the lack of a backboard.*

The first basketball team, consisting of nine players and their coach, on the steps of the Springfield College gym in 1891. James Naismith, dressed in street clothes, is in the middle row.

father, George Gabler, was playing the game before Naismith came to Springfield.

Gabler was a Holyoke physician and YMCA instructor who taught an exercise class for businessmen in the late 1800s. The class divided into two teams, and the players threw a round ball into peach baskets nailed to the wall. Stepladders were used to retrieve the ball from the baskets.

Ms. Gabler isn't certain her father actually invented basketball, only that he introduced the game to Naismith. A college chum from McGill University, Naismith paid a visit to the Gabler household for dinner in 1891 and observed the game then. To Ms. Gabler's thinking, Naismith ought to get credit for popularizing basketball, but not inventing it.

"I think Naismith stole my father's glory," Ms. Gabler said. "I think he should have said he changed an important part of the game. Every time I see a paper in Springfield saying basketball originated there — it's a big lie."

While the notion that basketball was played by Dr. Gabler is widely believed around Holyoke, there is no documentation for Ms. Gabler's claim. Her father requested that nothing be said while he was still alive, and later the Holyoke YMCA records were burned in a fire.

Anyone for a Game of Mintonette?

Like basketball, volleyball was the inspiration of a Massachusetts YMCA director.

In 1891, William G. Morgan, of Holyoke, Massachusetts, began experimenting with a less strenuous indoor game suitable for older men who did not want to run up and down the basketball court.

Originally, the game was called "mintonette," and Morgan envisioned it as a larger-than-life version of badminton. The game was first demonstrated in 1895, at a YMCA directors' conference held in Springfield, Massachusetts. A lawn tennis net was suspended high above the floor, and Morgan used the bladder of a soccer ball during the first game. Wisely, an associate named Dr. A. T. Halsted suggested changing mintonette to the snappier sounding volleyball because the ball is volleyed back and forth across the net. Marketing is everything.

Volleyball rules were published in 1897, and the first YMCA national tournament was held in 1922. Today, volleyball is an international sport, especially popular in the Orient, largely as a result of G.I.s bringing the game to the Pacific during World War II. The volleyball nets went up almost as soon as a beachhead was secured on such islands as Guam and the Philippines. The first world championships were played in 1949, and volleyball entered the Olympics in 1952.

William G. Morgan

Men playing volleyball at the Holyoke, Massachusetts, YMCA, where the game began. This photo was taken in the 1940s.

Grand Old Man of the Midway

In this photo taken in April 1930, Coach Stagg begins football try-outs at the University of Chicago with a pep talk. At the time of the photograph, Stagg had been coaching at the university for thirty-nine years.

In 1888, Walter Camp, the famous football coach from Yale, persuaded the rules committee to allow tackling below the waist, but not below the knees. When the Yale players had difficulty adapting to the new rule, an end by the name of Amos Alonzo Stagg had an idea. Stagg rolled a mattress into the rough shape of a body and hung it from the gym roof. He then laid other mattresses below it for cushions, and the team ran through tackling drills. Stagg had just invented the tackling dummy.

It was not the last innovation for this remarkable football player and coach, who was often referred to as the "Grand Old Man of the Midway." Over his fifty-seven-year coaching career, Stagg won 314 games. He is credited with inventing the end-around, the hidden-ball trick, the double reverse, the huddle, the quarterback keeper, wind sprints, the blocking sled, and the padded goal post. "All football comes from Stagg," Knute Rockne once claimed.

Born to a poor cobbler in West Orange, New Jersey, in 1862, Stagg came to fame as a baseball pitcher for Yale, first as an undergraduate and later as a divinity student studying for the Presbyterian ministry. While playing football for Yale, in 1889, he was named to Walter Camp's first All-America football team, though he stood only five feet six inches and weighed 160 pounds. Then after pitching Yale to five straight Big Three Championships, Stagg was offered forty-five hundred dollars to play baseball for the New York Giants. He turned it down because ball parks had saloons in them. A paragon of clean living, Stagg was a foe of smoking, drinking, and nightclubs; the strongest epithet he is said to have uttered was jackass, though rumor has it on occasion he said "double jackass." Stagg was so forthright he once ordered back a touchdown scored by his own team because the ball carrier had stepped out of bounds, albeit unnoticed by the officials. "I would like to be thought of as an honest man," Stagg commented.

When a friend suggested that he would never amount to much of a preacher, Stagg chose to "trade the pulpit for the athletic field, and make the young men of America my ministry." In 1890, he began his career as head coach at Springfield College, where his players were the first to

Left: *The caption on this dramatic engraving of an early football game reads, "And like a flash went round the end."*

FOOTNOTE TO BOWLING HISTORY

On July 26, 1850, John Taggart of Roxbury, Massachusetts, was issued patent #94,893 for a bowling ball covered with a rubber coating. The idea, according to Taggart's application, was a quieter ball. "[T]he great noise attendant upon the rolling of [the balls] along the alley, is very unpleasant. . . . A ball constructed in this manner . . . moves over the alley with very little noise."

An artist's rendering of an early game of bowling.

practice under lights. In 1891, Springfield played the first game under lights against Yale. Stagg was the first coach afforded professorial status when he was hired in 1892 at the University of Chicago. There he remained until 1932, when at the age of seventy he was asked to retire. Stagg coached another fourteen years at the College of the Pacific. His theories about clean living apparently paid off. Stagg died in Stockton, California, on March 17, 1965, at the age of 103.

Candlepin Bowling
More Popular Than Basketball?

In 1958, Boston's Channel 5 launched a Saturday candlepin bowling show that it hopefully dubbed "Fun for All Ages." To the wonderment and chagrin of those who had predicted the show was certain to be the video equivalent of the Edsel, stupefying numbers of black-and-white Zeniths and Motorolas were tuned in to it each week. The show is now broadcast in color, and its name has been changed to "Candlepin Bowling," but it is otherwise just about the same as it was when Ike was in the

White House and is just as popular. Every week, between 150,000 and 180,000 households tune in, considerably more than watch a Boston Celtics regular season game and more than double the draw for a match between the Red Sox and the dreaded Yankees. Only during the football play-offs does "Candlepin Bowling" occasionally slip to the #2 spot.

Had the naysayers done their homework, they would have discovered what is obvious today: Yankees love bowling. Consider this 1891 item published in the Hartford *Courant:* "There was a lively time at Koch's alley on Temple Street last night, and the rumble of the big wooden balls . . . disturbed the slumber of the officers on duty at police headquarters across the way. It was the second night of the bowling tournament, and excitement ran riot."

The style of bowling that dominates Massachusetts, Maine, and New Hampshire, and that is virtually unknown anywhere else, began in 1880 when Vermont native Justin White bought out a friend's saloon/bowling hall in Worcester, Massachusetts. He removed the ponderous pins and replaced them with sawed-off broomsticks. The candlepin ball, is about the size of a softball and weighs as much as a brickbat, or up to two pounds, seven ounces — roughly the same as a single candlepin.

The reasons for candlepin popularity have eluded many of the region's deepest thinkers. The most succinct explanation is offered by Florence Greenleaf and Paul Tedford. "The urge to hurl something at an object is as old as humankind and is today still inherent in the makeup of

The Pilgrims brought the sport of bowling with them to the New World.

65

human beings," the authors of *The Game of Candlepin Bowling* write. "What was once a necessity among prehistoric men to stun animal life for the purpose of bodily sustenance has now become a high form of recreation."

And you probably thought it was just fun.

A Chaste Diversion for Ladies

In 1760, Joseph Merlin made a dramatic entrance at a prestigious ball at the London home of a Mrs. Cornelly. Bowing a priceless violin, Merlin rolled into the ballroom strapped into his latest invention, roller skates. Unfortunately, Merlin had figured out neither how to stop nor how to turn the skates, and he crashed into a great gilded mirror worth more than five hundred pounds. The roller skate's reputation would not recover until January of 1863, when James Plimpton patented the guidable parlor skate, a maneuverable skate that launched a fad.

Plimpton was a Massachusetts furniture salesman with a natural mechanical genius. In the winter of 1860–61, on the advice of his doctor, he took up ice skating. When warm weather brought an end to his

Above: Some early roller skates. *Near right:* A couple skating, from an advertisement, c. 1880. *Far right:* Trade cards, which were simply decorative handouts from manufacturers, added to the excitement over skating in the 1880s.

66

THE
Vineyard Roller Skating Rink.

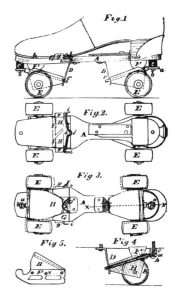

Left: *Roller-skating rink on Martha's Vineyard, 1879.* Top: *Patent drawings, 1863.*

exercise, Plimpton began to seek a way to permit skating all year round. "Pennie parlor skates" were popular then with children, but like Merlin's invention, they could not be controlled.

Plimpton solved this problem with two pairs of metal casters set beneath the heel and toe. With an arrangement of metal washers and an India rubber ball between each roller assembly and the footplate, the inventor had only to shift his weight to control the skate.

In 1868, after introducing roller skates to the socially prominent in New York and Newport, Plimpton launched a well-planned marketing campaign. He would visit a city, rent a hall, and send out engraved invitations to the local elite. With the interest of the top hat set aroused, the support of the rest of the community was presumably assured. Plimpton would then sell a franchise and move on. His skates were leased at a set annual fee.

Plimpton had more in mind than profit. He had a social and moral vision. Rollerskating, conducted within the proper environment, would be an unchaperoned but chaste diversion from which secluded Victorian women might especially benefit. The rinks were carefully regulated to produce an environment conducive to physical grace, good health, mental acuity, and genteel behavior. Flashy advertising, liquor, and tobacco were banned from Plimpton's rinks, as were shouting, the admission of "objectionable persons," and even musical accompaniment without special permission. By 1871, rollerskating had become a national craze — the California rights to a Plimpton franchise purchased for four thousand dollars resold for thirty-six. After defending himself in patent infringement cases in England, Plimpton conquered Europe. In 1876, at the age

James Plimpton

67

of forty-eight, he was the absolute monarch of a skating empire.

The sun was soon to set. When his factory in Brooklyn, already producing two thousand pairs of skates a week, could not keep up with the demand, Plimpton turned to Samuel Winslow, a Worcester ice skate manufacturer, to produce skates at two dollars a pair. In 1880, when Plimpton's original patent expired, Winslow immediately began manufacturing roller skates of his own design. Like P. T. Barnum, Winslow saw nothing wrong with hype, hoopla, or loutish behavior; he eventually became the largest manufacturer of roller skates in the world.

At Last, the Wooden Golf Tee

When the first Scottish and Dutch golfers teed up, they scooped up a handful of dirt, molded it into a small mound, and set the ball on it. With few variations — the introduction of sand over dirt for instance, with a bucket of water for cleanliness — this method was good enough for four centuries.

But since most golfers spend more time than they would care to in the sand, they eventually tired of teeing off from it, and improvements came along. In the 1890s, rubber tees began to appear, and in 1895, British manufacturers offered paper tees with golf balls. One golf magazine said of them, "We doubt if they are likely to meet with general acceptance. . . ."

The most important step forward came in 1899, when Dr. George F. Grant of Boston obtained a patent for the first modern wood tee. Dr. Grant was a graduate of Harvard University's second class in dentistry in 1870, and he became a leading authority on the cleft palate. When he was not practicing dentistry, he loved to play golf. However, he got "darned tired" of scooping out sand to make mounds every time he was ready to tee his ball, and so he developed his wooden tee. It is described in the patent as "a golf-tee comprising a tapering portion to be driven in the ground first, and a flexible tabular head, the lower end of which embraces the upper portion of the base." Dr. Grant gave away his tees and made no attempt to promote them.

Another dentist, Dr. William Lowell, of Maplewood, New Jersey, also patented a wooden tee. Lowell, like Grant, had no real interest in marketing his invention. Lowell, however, had business-minded sons, and in 1920, the Reddy Tee was born. When Walter Hagen began using the tees in 1923, they swept across the fairways of the world.

As this engraving by A. B. Frost (c. 1900) shows, golfers teed off from a mound of dirt, until the 1920 invention of the Reddy Tee.

Golfers

While the New Jersey dentist receives credit for popularizing Dr. Grant's idea, he couldn't have done it without some Yankee input. The first tees were turned in Norway, Maine, from the best white birch lumber available.

THE LUMINESCENT GOLF BALL

As any true duffer will testify, there is no such thing as too much golf. Which might explain why Nelson and Corky Newcomb, a father-and-son team from Mirror Lake, New Hampshire, invented the glow-in-the-dark golf ball. A translucent, hard plastic sphere has a thin cylindrical hole molded into it. The golfer inserts a small luminescent nightstick that glows for about six hours. Whether or not night golf will catch on is another story.

The King of Fly Dope

One day in the summer of 1962 a man named Irving Stevens was fishing in the Moosehead Lake region of Maine at a place called Shirley Bog. The bog was nasty with black flies, but Stevens had spent much of his life around the woods and had come prepared. He never ventured out without a pint jar of his own fly dope, a foul-smelling, oily concoction of pine tar, citronella, and mineral oil. On this day he noticed

Irving Stevens

a woman and five children trying to fish but being forced by the flies to retreat to their station wagon.

"What are you using for fly dope?" he inquired. The woman said she had nothing. So Irving let her and the kids slather up with his.

Irving never learned the woman's name, but she thanked him as if he had saved her life. It got him to thinking: If he could give the stuff away, why not try to sell it?

He promptly mixed up some more — a home-brew that once was carried by every Maine woodsman before the convenience and generally superior effectiveness of chemical sprays and lotions made it obsolete. He bought some two-ounce bottles, had a local printer make some labels featuring a moose, and pondered on a name. Irving, he reasoned, was easy to remember. He took a few bottles of Irving's Fly Dope to the Western Auto in Corinna, Maine, and took some more to the machine shop where he worked. Though the first bottles leaked, they sold.

Irving became the king of fly dope. His plant — the back bedroom of an 1830 Cape that had seen better days — was stuffed with jars, bottles, and bottle caps. Here Irving mixed his concoction in a five-gallon spring-water jar and then heated it on top of the stove. The smell, strong enough to ward off black flies, permeated the house. It goes without saying that fly dope production and marriage were mutually exclusive: Irving was a lifelong bachelor.

Irving sold his concoction to country stores and gas stations throughout northern New England. Without an advertising budget, he created "anecdopes," jingles that would catch the buyer's eye:

> Didn't have the strength to cope
> And ward off a nasty sting
> Until he bought Irving's Fly Dope
> And heard the fat lady sing.

"It must be good," Irving once commented. "People still buy it."

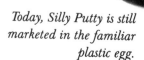

Today, Silly Putty is still marketed in the familiar plastic egg.

Golly, Look at It Bounce

In the early 1940s, James Wright, an engineer then working at General Electric's New Haven, Connecticut, laboratory, was assigned to develop a product of the utmost importance to the war effort: an inexpensive substitute for rubber. What he came up with instead was Silly Putty.

The U.S. War Production Board had approached GE with the idea of using chemically synthesized rubber in the mass production of jeep and airplane tires, gas masks, and a wide variety of military gear.

Working with boric acid and silicone oil, Wright succeeded in creating a rubber-like compound with highly unusual properties. Rolled into a ball, it bounced higher than anything else on the market; left alone it flowed until it was flat as a pancake. You could roll it, stretch it, and hit it with a hammer. Best of all, it lifted an image when pressed across newspaper print or the comics.

"Astounding," one scientist is said to have commented after a demonstration. "What's it really good for?"

"Well," a chemist replied thoughtfully, "you can use it to roll, drop on the floor, and say 'Golly, look at it bounce.'"

"Bouncing putty" had no real industrial advantages. In their frustration, GE engineers often entertained themselves for hours, but what could you do with it? No one seemed to know.

That was still the situation in 1949 when Ruth Fallgatter, a toy store owner in New Haven, attended a party where Wright was present. A wad of bouncing putty was the hit of the party. At the time, Fallgatter was putting together a toy catalogue with the help of Peter Hodgson, an advertising copywriter who had recently moved to New Haven from Montreal, and the two included the putty. It outsold all the other items in the catalogue.

Nonetheless, Fallgatter was unimpressed. So Hodgson bought a large mass of the stuff from General Electric for $147 and hired a Yale student to separate it into one-ounce balls. He marketed Silly Putty inside

Cartoonist Henry Boltinoff drew this rendering of Silly Putty's introduction to the scientific community for Collier's Magazine, *December 2, 1944.*

colored plastic eggs and sold them for $1 a piece. Mass-marketed, Silly Putty became an overnight success, racking up sales in the millions of dollars a year. Upon his death, Hodgson's estate was worth nearly $140 million.

Scientists have finally found by-products for the silicone-based putty in plastic surgery.

Remember the Pluto Platter?

Sometime in the 1870s, William Russell Frisbie opened a bakery in Bridgeport, Connecticut. His specialty was a line of homemade pies baked in circular tin pans and sugar cookies packaged in tin containers with circular lids. "Frisbie" was stamped in the tin tops and pie bottoms. According to legend, the Frisbie factory was near the Yale University campus, and in the 1920s, tossing the tin pans was something of a fad. Students tossed the metal pie tins and yelled "Frisbie!" the way golfers yell "Fore!"

On the other side of the country, a California carpenter and building inspector named Walter Frederick Morrison began tinkering in his basement with "tenite," a plastic compound from Eastman Kodak used in making extrusion parts. Morrison, the son of the inventor of the sealed headlight, was fascinated by flight. He carved a plastic disk that very much resembled the Frisbie pie tins. The essential difference was the slight aerodynamic slope of the modern Frisbee and the curled lip, which enhanced stability. He called his invention the "Lil' Abner," and in the

Above: *The Frisbie pie tins that started the Frisbee craze.* Right: *The management of the Frisbie Pie Company posing in front of the plant, c. 1920.*

late forties and early fifties, he and his wife sold them at county fairs.

As a gimmick, Morrison claimed he was selling invisible string. "Watch me slide this disk along the invisible string," he would tell the crowds and toss the toy to his wife. A Lil' Abner came free with every purchase of invisible string.

Word of Morrison's creation finally reached Spud Melin and Rich Knerr in 1957. The pair were back-yard manufacturers of slingshots. Wham-O, their company, was named after the sound of a high-speed object striking a wall. They bought the rights to the Lil' Abner and, in an effort to capitalize on the country's fascination with flying saucers, renamed the toy the "Pluto Platter." Planets were embossed around the outside of the ring along with instructions to "Play Catch! Invent Games!" Like the Hula Hoop, the Pluto Platter was an instant sensation on college campuses. A year later, the name was changed to "Frisbee," after the pie company that started it all a century earlier.

The Frisbee has had an enduring popularity. Such was the fascination with the new toy that in 1968 the navy spent nearly four hundred thousand dollars testing the Frisbee as a vehicle for keeping flares aloft for extended periods of time. The navy also developed a mechanical Frisbee launcher.

The Checkered Game of Life

In 1860, Milton Bradley opened a lithography business in a small office opposite Court Square in Springfield, Massachusetts. Lithography was a new process then, and Bradley was so depressed by the sorry state of his business that he postponed the date of his wedding. When he complained of his troubles to George Tapley, a close friend in the bookbinding business, Tapley tried to cheer him up. "Let's play a game," he suggested.

That night, the pair played an old English game on a board with oval disks. Bradley had a wonderful time. Before he left that night, he had decided to invent a game that he would lithograph and package in his own plant.

The Checkered Game of Life was both a technical and marketing masterpiece. The game used a checkerboard pattern, with instructions for advancing on the light squares, since those could be printed on. In keeping with the spirit of Puritanism, neither dice nor cards were involved in this family-oriented game — both were considered forms of

Milton Bradley

73

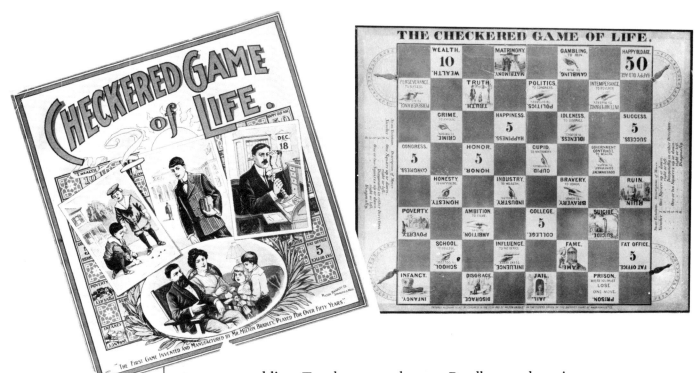

In the early 1900s, the Checkered Game of Life, the first board game, was still selling strong, even after fifty years.

gambling. To advance each man, Bradley used a spinner.

The object of the game was also a lesson in morality. The winner attempted to reach "Happy Old Age" through clean living rather than the ignominy of "Ruin." It reflected the Puritanical belief that our futures are governed to a great extent by the voluntary actions of our pasts. While a player now and then found circumstances that compelled a course greatly to his disadvantage, he probably put himself there through some wrong move in the early part of the game. "You are the captain of your own ship, master of your destiny" seemed to be the inherent message.

Bradley and one of his assistants packaged several hundred of the games and left for New York. At the first stationery store Bradley visited on Broadway, he sold the arm load of samples he had walked in with. By the end of the second day, his trunk of games was empty. That winter, Bradley sold forty thousand copies of The Checkered Game of Life. The inventor was so encouraged by his success that he and his fiancée set the date for their wedding.

About the time repeat orders for the new game began to trickle in, Abraham Lincoln was nominated for the presidency. A friend of Bradley's convinced him that a color lithograph of the next president would be an instant success. Bradley turned out a portrait of Lincoln — without his beard. All was going well until it was learned that Lincoln had ceased shaving. Sales came to a halt.

Stopping by Bradley's office, George Tapley again tried to cheer up his friend. "Let's play another game," Tapley suggested.

In 1960, an updated version of The Checkered Game of Life was introduced to mark the one hundredth anniversary of the board game. Originally, the object of the game was simply to achieve "Happy Old Age" through clean living. The goal in the new version: to become a millionaire.

The Godfather of Video Games

Forget Atari, Bally, and all those other companies you thought were responsible for the invention of the video game. "The Godfather of Video Games," as he has been called, is Ralph H. Baer, a sixty-seven-year-old engineer at Sanders, the defense contractor located in Nashua, New Hampshire. If you have any doubts, just ask him. "In case after case," says Baer, who has frequently represented Sanders on the witness stand in patent litigation, "the courts have ruled in our favor. Even the coin-operated games go squarely back to what we did in 1967."

What Baer did, according to an official notebook dated September 1, 1966, was ask the question: What can you do with a television set besides turn it on and off? At the time, there were more than sixty million television sets in the United States alone. For a consumer products engineer, a Jewish immigrant who had escaped from Nazi Germany and first learned electronics from a radio repair course, that represented a lot of potential customers. The answer came to him while sitting in a bus terminal in New York: play games. "The first thing that came into my head," Baer recalls, "is that it should sell for $19.95."

Back in New Hampshire, Baer set to work in his spare time. By December he had devised a crude game similar in concept to Pac Man: One spot chased another spot around on the screen. Sanders, he admits, was not thrilled initially about one of their leading engineers playing games rather than working on the important business of military defense. But after a company executive played with an electronic shooting gallery Baer and his associates had devised, Baer was given the go-ahead. He and two other engineers worked in secret in a room on the sixth floor. By early 1967, they had a basic paddle and ball game; by the end of that year, they were playing hockey. Patent #3,659,285 was issued on April 25, 1972, to Baer and his associates, William T. Rusch and William L. Harrison.

That same spring, Sanders licensed the technology to Magnavox: Baer was off on only one of his early estimates. "Odyssey," the home video game package introduced by Magnavox, sold for $99.95 — considerably more than Baer's $19.95. But it sold some one hundred thousand games. The following year, when Atari brought out a licensed home video game sold through Sears, the industry took off. Today, video game sales are in excess of $10 billion a year.

Ralph Baer, inventor of video games.

CHAPTER FOUR

Dollars To Doughnuts

Of Chocolate Chip Cookies &
Other Necessities of Life

The Quintessential New Englander

When Fannie Farmer died seventy years ago, her name was a house-hold word — literally. It adorned a cookbook that had already been a best-seller for two decades, sitting reassuringly on countertops and inside cupboards. Even today, about three million copies later, people who have never even boiled water know her name.

Fannie Merritt Farmer was born in Boston on March 23, 1857. She grew up in nearby Medford, where as a teenager she experienced a stroke or suffered an illness that left her with a pronounced limp. Housebound, she became fascinated with cooking. It soon was apparent that hers was no ordinary skill in the kitchen; those close to her urged her to train for a career teaching cooking.

In 1887, when she was about thirty, she entered the Boston Cooking School, already an institution of repute. Farmer's energy, her practical experience, and her mix of logical and intuitive skills must have burst into flower in that congenial atmosphere. She had scarcely graduated in 1889 when she was asked to return as assistant to the principal. Two years later, Miss Farmer was principal.

Farmer's view that cooking should be as much a science as an art caught up early with the casual measurements of the time. Directions were then given in approximates: rounded teaspoons (any old teaspoon would do), heaping cups (whatever its size), a walnut-sized lump of this, a dab of that. It is said that while Farmer was teaching, a little girl, whose name in almost every version of the tale is Marcia, observed that the heaped teaspoon called for could turn out to be a different quantity each time. Miss Farmer was delighted with this bit of precocity and promptly invented the level measurement.

For Farmer, the level measure became a crusade. In her cookbooks, and indeed every time she put pen to paper, the admonition to scrupulous measurement was repeated. "Correct measurements are absolutely necessary to insure the best results," she wrote in her famous book.

The famous book, of course, is *The Boston Cooking-School Cook Book*, first published in 1896, and eventually to be known around the world simply as *The Fannie Farmer Cookbook*. Besides featuring hundreds of clearly written recipes, it was crammed with brisk information, chemical expositions, culinary physics, the physiology of flesh and fish, how-to's and ways-of, charts and tables, household hints, lists of menus, and at the end a prospectus of the cooking school's offerings. She took it to Boston's most respectable publishers, Little, Brown and Company, who first

These young Victorian ladies are learning a scientific approach to the culinary arts at a normal school, or teacher's college.

Fannie Merritt Farmer

turned it down. But by agreeing to pay for the printing, she persuaded them to bring out three thousand copies. It became one of the all-time best-sellers, went through twelve revisions, innumerable printings, and in a very altered form is still in print today.

Why was it so popular? Certainly it had competitors. What captured and held the imagination and loyalty of millions of cooks was the mind and personality of its author found on every page. That richly complex woman is reflected in its variety, its clarity, its breadth, its stern passion, and the strength of character that underlies it like New England granite.

In 1902, after eleven years as principal of the Boston Cooking School, Farmer opened Miss Farmer's School of Cookery to provide cooking instruction for individuals rather than teachers. From 1905 to 1915, she also wrote a monthly food column in the *Woman's Home Companion*. And all during this time, Farmer was turning out other books, although none of them had the success and fame of her first.

Fannie Farmer died on January 15, 1915. The *Woman's Home Companion* couldn't bring itself to give the bad news to its readers and ran her columns for the next eleven months without mentioning that they were posthumous. Farmer's last column contained many of the staunch New England dishes that had come to be associated with her. Among them were Boston baked beans, steamed brown bread, baked and stuffed haddock, Indian pudding, and salt codfish balls. It was a fitting farewell.

The Glory of Baked Beans

The bean pot, that homely, all-purpose, ovenproof, thick-as-a-brick jug which most of us keep on a shelf in the basement or at the back of a kitchen cabinet, is more than just another pot. It is the coat of arms of the Yankee kitchen. (Imagine what humiliation Kentuckians must suffer, known to all the world by a throwaway cardboard bucket full of fried chicken.)

People in other regions of the country are proud of their own ways with beans. But generally speaking, most other people — like Tex-Mex cooks — think of beans as a second-rate meal or a companion to something better. Only in New England is Saturday night reserved for eating Boston baked beans and only beans, with nothing else needed to complete the picture save a loaf of steamed brown bread and relish on the side.

Like Thanksgiving turkey and corn-on-the-cob, baked beans were probably a gift from the Indians. They mixed a slab of bear fat into a clay pot full of beans, then buried the pot for the rest of the day in a hole in the earth on top of a heap of heated rocks. Most historians contend that the Indians sweetened their beans with maple syrup.

Nothing beats a hearty bowl of beans after a hard day driving logs downriver. These men are taking their rest in 1901 after a log drive down the Swift and Webb rivers.

79

A baked bean supper held on the Boston Common, May 20, 1950.

Though dedicated outdoorsmen still make their beans in a bean hole, the classic place to do it is in the iron-doored brick oven at the side of the hearth; it's naturally hot there — but not "too" hot. Some fanatics contend that a wood fire is the only proper heat source for baking beans because only wood imparts the proper flavor. "Remember, baked beans began outdoors, in bean holes of lumber camps, in the tall woods. And the taste of the forest is essential in them still," Robert P. Tristram Coffin wrote in *Mainstays of Maine,* published in 1944. Coffin suggested those without a wood stove beseech their better-equipped neighbors to bake their beans for them ("It is the best New England test of a Christian!"). Indeed there was a time when bakers would travel through town early Saturday morning, pick up family bean pots, bring them to the stone hearth of a community oven, then return the pots full of baked beans in time for supper.

Despite their celebrated status, New England baked beans are simpler than any other and clear of purpose: Jacob's cattle, yellow-eye, kidney, or soldier beans are soaked overnight. Then a couple of slices of salt pork are added. Brown sugar, maple syrup, or molasses is used for the sweetener. Maybe an onion, a sprinkle of dry mustard, or a dash of ginger, salt, and pepper are added. And that's it.

To make a real Saturday night supper, you also need brown bread — Boston brown bread steamed in a cylinder mold and sliced with a

80

string held taut between the hands. A spoonful of piccalilli and a scoop of cole slaw are the only decoration this luscious combination requires. It is a meal of simple foods, frumpy yet seductive. In fact, the only thing better than Saturday night beans might be a baked bean breakfast on Sunday morning.

Eating Plain & Square

When it comes to eating plain and square, the Northeast has got the plainest, squarest, clunkiest, and most wonderful meat and potatoes meal in America — the New England Boiled Dinner. What could be simpler than a big hunk of corned beef brisket, surrounded by a rainbow of vegetables: beets in a crimson puddle, limp cabbage wedges, small boiled potatoes, and heavy rutabagas. Even the name is prosaic.

Americans did not invent it. English boiled beef goes way back. But it is rightfully New England's own because its essential qualities are common sense and logic — throw everything into the pot and pull it out when it is cooked. Boiled dinner is as frugal, Spartan, and pridefully common as a native Vermont dairy farmer.

The anchor to the dish is beef brisket, corned. Before corned briskets were available in every supermarket in vacuum-sealed bags, cooks had to cure their own, submerging the beef for weeks in a brine made from salt and gunpowder; the latter was contained in shells known as "corns," hence the name. Properly corned, the beef had plenty of tang to flavor the pot of water and all the vegetables thrown in.

On this side of the Atlantic, boiled dinner, like a good dog, assumed the personality of the region. In Maine, it is said, cooks prefer the rump or flank to the brisket, and some early cookbooks even call for centerpieces other than corned beef. Recipes survive for salt pork in lieu of beef. The pork is dusted with cinnamoned flour and browned until the fat is rendered. Closer to the shore, there are aberrant oceanic boiled dinners centered on codfish; farther south the centerpiece is boiled chicken. In his authoritative book *American Cookery,* James Beard suggests studding the brisket with cloves after it has been boiled, then glazing it with maple syrup. Beard also says that potatoes were not part of the repertoire until 1725, when they were introduced to New England by Scotch-Irish settlers.

Sad to say, our simple meal has languished in culinary obscurity for centuries, save one brief moment in 1885 when Grover Cleveland made it the supper of choice in the White House. Cleveland assumed the presi-

President Grover Cleveland made corn beef and cabbage the supper of choice in the White House.

dency from Chester A. Arthur, who regularly dined on foie gras, charlotte russe, and macaroni pie "with oysters" and insisted that everything be called by its French name.

A regular "Joe," the president put up with the folderol until one night he caught a whiff of corned beef and cabbage being eaten by the servants. Cleveland traded his Arthurian meal for theirs. "It was the best dinner I had had for months," he later beamed. *"Boef corne au cabeau!"*

The Native Cranberry

As corny as it sounds, cranberries are as American as apple pie. Maybe more so. The apple was an immigrant. Along with the blueberry and the Concord grape, the cranberry, or *Vaccinium macrocarpon,* is native to North America. And nowhere is it more native than Massachusetts, where it was named, domesticated, and turned into juice. Today, over half of the nation's cranberry crop is produced in the Bay State.

The Indians, who used them for medicines, dyes, and food, introduced cranberries to the first settlers. The native term, "sassamanesh," was replaced when some forgotten Pilgrim noticed the pink, hooked blossoms produced in July and was reminded of a crane. Later, the crane was shortened to cran.

We do not know whether or not the Pilgrims established the tradition of cranberries and turkey at the first Thanksgiving, but by 1708, when President Leverett was installed at Harvard, cranberries were a popular dish. None of the delights of that day, Leverett wrote, ". . . exceeded . . . the serving of beauteous cranberries."

The Father of Cranberry Cultivation was Henry Hall, a sea captain and jack-of-all-trades from Dennis, Massachusetts. According to folklore, sometime between 1812 and 1816 Hall noticed that when sand blew across the wild vines near the edge of water they produced better fruit the next year. "If nature can do it, why can't I?" Hall asked. From that observation, he developed the modern cranberry bog and cranberry cultivation. From then on, the fruit became a staple of holiday dinners all along the South Shore and Cape Cod. By 1900, using Hall's method, more than twenty-five thousand acres of cranberries were under cultivation.

It was not until 1912, however, that cranberries were introduced to the nation at large, thanks to the efforts of Marcus L. Urann. In those

Cranberry harvesters, late 1880s.

days, cranberries were sold fresh in the fall. Whatever had not moved by Christmas went out the door in a dumpster. Urann, a practical lawyer from South Hanson, Massachusetts, with a "can do" attitude, was appalled by the portion of the annual crop that ended up on the compost heap. He came up with the idea of a mass-produced canned cranberry sauce that tasted as good as homemade. That fall, he stirred his first batch of Ocean Spray Cape Cod Cranberry Sauce and founded the Ocean Spray Preserving Company.

Urann's idea did not go unnoticed. By 1930, three powerful growers were struggling for control of the market. Eventually, they settled their differences and formed the cooperative known today as Ocean Spray Cranberries, Inc. In 1963, an Ocean Spray chemist suggested a sweetened version of cranberry juice, and cranberries became a year-round product. Today, Ocean Spray represents 85 percent of the cranberry crop and sells more than 90 million gallons of cranberry juice and millions of containers of cranberry sauce annually.

Who Put the Hole in the Doughnut?

Captain Hanson Crockett Gregory

Life is full of intriguing mysteries such as which came first: the chicken or the egg? Or who put the hole in the doughnut? We do not know the answer to the first, but without question, Hanson Crockett Gregory, a Maine sea captain born in 1832, was responsible for the second. The name of his ship, the *Frypan,* befits a man whose achievement is a monument to grease.

According to the short, prosaic version of the tale, as a boy, Captain Gregory often watched his mother prepare "fried cakes," marveling that the centers never got cooked. One day in 1847, he poked a hole through the center of the cake with a fork, and the doughnut hole was born.

That said, we prefer the longer, more dramatic version of the story, in which Gregory was on a sea voyage in 1847, and the *Frypan* was being buffeted by high winds, powerful waves, and a Biblical rain. In the heat of the battle, several of the crew were injured, and the remaining sailors were risking life and limb to bring the vessel to port. As Gregory battled to keep the ship on course, the cook brought him one of his beloved fried cakes for sustenance.

Just then, the *Frypan* was struck by a mountainous wave. Not wishing to lose his doughnut, the captain jammed it down over one of the spokes and gripped the wheel with both hands. When the wave sub-

sided, there was the doughnut, safe, sound, and ready to eat.

After the ship finally returned to Camden, the cook proudly exhibited his new doughnut. It created such a stir among seafaring men that other captains required their cooks to produce similar doughnuts, and a tradition was born. Twenty-five years later, John F. Blondel of Thomaston, Maine, received a patent for the first doughnut hole machine. A spring pushed the dough out of a center tube to form the hole.

Needless to say, not everyone accepted the story of Gregory's contribution to gastronomy. The Wampanoag Indian tribe, for instance, claimed one of their ancestors created the first doughnut hole when an arrow meant for a Pilgrim housewife went astray and pierced a fried cake she was making. The controversy was settled definitively on October 27, 1941, at the Great Doughnut Debate, sponsored by the National Dunking Association. The participants were Fred Crockett, a great-grandnephew of Captain Gregory, and Chief High Eagle. The judges swallowed Crockett's story whole. On November 2, 1947, one hundred years after that momentous voyage, a bronze plaque commemorating the birthplace of Gregory was placed in Glen Cove, Rockport, Maine.

The Poet of Bran

Reverend Sylvester Graham

The Reverend Sylvester Graham believed in all things regular. In the mid-1800s, Graham, a former Presbyterian minister from West Suffield, Connecticut, plagued by chronic ill health, married his nurse and advocated spirituality through healthy nutrition and temperance. For home baking, he recommended using his own special flour, a grind of

whole wheat that retained the bran, thus anticipating the great concern for regularity that surfaced in Victorian times.

Though his philosophy was controversial (Ralph Waldo Emerson once called Graham the "poet of bran"), Graham did have an influential following. Joseph Smith, founder of the Mormon Church, Thomas Edison, and Horace Greeley were all said to believe in Graham. His adherents were known as Grahamites, and their lives were based on Grahamology, a strict philosophy of grace through a diet of vegetables and water. Many of the tenets of Grahamology would sound familiar today: He derided the consumption of red meat, alcohol, white bread, and fatty oils; he believed strongly in exercise, frequent bathing, and brushing the teeth regularly. So influential were his theories about baking that commercial bakers in Boston protested the public appearances where Graham expounded his views. Eventually the bakers capitulated and profited by baking graham crackers and bran bread. In a roundabout way, Graham's belief in a cold breakfast of brans and milk led to the development of the breakfast cereal industry.

Graham's philosophy led to some unusual practices. Fats, Graham believed, heated the libido and led to sexual excesses. The ingestion of condiments, such as mustard, ketchup, and pepper, led to insanity. At the Battle Creek Sanitarium, one of many institutes based on Grahamology, patients with high blood pressure were fed up to fourteen pounds of grapes a day; thin patients were fed up to twenty-six times a day and kept still to conserve calories.

In spite of a regular diet of healthy foods, Graham lived only to the age of fifty-seven. His theories had more longevity. Well known by the 1880s, the graham cracker is still one of America's favorite cookies. Graham flour, still on the market today, is usually a coarse grind of whole wheat. The graham cracker crust, a blend of cracker crumbs, sugar, and melted butter, is a ubiquitous presence at church suppers, bridge parties, and other special occasions. Whether any of the fillings would meet Graham's approval is another question.

Parker House Rolls

In Boston, Parker House means "hotel," but to the rest of the country it means "rolls," thanks to a German baker named Ward who first made the delicate dinner roll in the late 1850s.

The crustless roll with the fold, the perfect spot for a pat of butter, was an instant success at the hotel, enjoyed by the likes of Ralph Waldo Emerson, John Greenleaf Whittier, Oliver Wendell Holmes, and other important men with multiple names. Soon, thousands of them were being made and shipped daily to hotels in cities as far west as Chicago. Not only were they consumed by the rich and famous, Parker House rolls were also made by some destined for world fame: Early in this century, a young Vietnamese student named Ho Chi Minh apprenticed in the Parker House pastry shop.

The Parker House no longer ships its famous rolls, but it still makes twelve thousand of them every week to serve in the dining rooms of the Boston landmark. Here is Baker Ward's original recipe, scaled down for home use.

An artist's rendering of Boston's Parker House, Pre-1896.

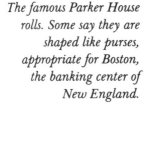

The famous Parker House rolls. Some say they are shaped like purses, appropriate for Boston, the banking center of New England.

SLICED BREAD

We are not sure if John Currier of Springfield, Massachusetts, is responsible for the phrase "It's the greatest thing since sliced bread." What we do know is that Currier invented one of the first bread slicers, patented in 1871.

Parker House Rolls

1 package (1 scant tablespoon) dry yeast	2½ teaspoons salt
¼ cup warm water	3 tablespoons butter
2 cups milk	3 cups all-purpose flour
2 tablespoons sugar	2½ to 3 cups additional flour
	Melted butter

In a large bowl, dissolve the yeast in the warm water. Combine the milk, sugar, salt, and butter in a saucepan; scald, then cool to lukewarm. Add to the yeast and stir. Add 3 cups of the flour and beat with a wooden spoon until smooth and creamy. Cover the bowl with plastic wrap or a damp towel and let rise in a warm spot for 1 hour, or until light and bubbly.

Add enough of the additional flour to make a soft dough. Knead for several minutes. Return the dough to a greased bowl and let rise again until doubled. Punch down; then roll the dough on a floured board into a rectangle ⅓ inch thick. Cut the dough into 3-inch squares and brush with melted butter. Stretch each square, fold over, and tuck under so the roll doesn't develop a "grin" when it bakes. Flatten slightly and place on buttered cookie sheets ⅛ inch apart. Let rise for 45 minutes, until almost doubled. Bake at 400°F. for 10 to 12 minutes. Remove from oven and brush with melted butter. Break apart to serve. Makes about 3 dozen.

Fried Clams? Just a Little Joke

On the reverse side of their wedding certificate, Lawrence and Bessie Woodman of Essex, Massachusetts, recorded the most significant events in their lives. The first two lines listed the birth dates of their two oldest sons, Wilbur and Henry. The third notation read, "We fried the first clam — in the town of Essex, July 3, 1916." Sure, others claimed to have fried a clam earlier than 1916, but no one has offered such incontrovertible evidence.

The invention of the fried clam was not the result of painstaking research on the Woodmans' part. Instead it came about as a result of what can best be described as "just a little joke."

Lawrence Woodman wanted to build a business he could pass on to his children. While a motorman on a trolley for the Massachusetts Electric Railway, he noticed people clamming along the coastline during his

round-trip runs between Gloucester and Salem. It occurred to him that clamming would be an excellent way to earn extra money. So Woodman opened a small stand on Main Street in Essex where on the weekends he and Bessie sold fruit, chewing gum, homemade potato chips, and fresh clams.

Until July 3, 1916, the concession stand was not the moneymaker the Woodmans hoped it would be; but after that date, their business dramatically improved. A fisherman from Gloucester named Tarr happened to be at the stand nibbling on potato chips while Woodman was complaining to a couple of other customers that "business was slower than a couple of snails headed uphill." Noticing a bucket of clams nearby, Tarr suggested the Woodmans try frying their clams.

"If they're half as tasty as those fried potato chips of yours," he opined, "you'll never have to worry about business again."

"That's ridiculous," one customer snapped, while another pointed out that "clams have shells." Embarrassed into silence, Tarr said he was only kidding. After the customers left, however, Woodman and his wife shucked a few clams, rolled them in batter, and fried them in the pan normally used for potato chips. A short time later, Woodman happened to spot Tarr across the street and served him the first plate of fried clams.

The next day was the Fourth, and Tarr suggested the Woodmans begin selling fried clams at the annual celebration. A year later, a Boston fish market advertised that it was "now equipped to serve the new taste treat — fried clams." Today, the Howard Johnson chain alone sells fried

Left: *Lawrence Woodman sits beside his stand where fried clams were introduced on July 4, 1916.*

clam dinners by the millions, and the Woodman stand is still in existence. When Lawrence Woodman passed away at the age of eighty-four, the town of Essex paid its respects to the father of the fried clam by lowering the flag at the town hall to half mast.

Ruth Wakefield

America's Favorite Cookie

In the olden days of 1933, baking chocolate came only in large slabs and not in chips, bits, or morsels. One day Mrs. Ruth Wakefield was making butter dewdrop cookies for the guests at her Toll House Inn in Whitman, Massachusetts. The recipe called for melted chocolate, but Mrs. Wakefield was running a bit late, so she decided to chop up the chocolate and let it melt into the cookies while they baked.

Instead, the chopped chocolate kept its integrity and, fortunately for everyone born since 1933, the chocolate chip cookie made its debut. Mrs. Wakefield called them chocolate crunch cookies at first, then changed the name to Toll House cookies. Chocolate manufacturers caught on and soon began selling bags of chocolate chips just for these cookies.

The Toll House Inn burned to the ground in 1984. Present owner Donald Saccone temporarily relocated to Abington, Massachusetts, and his Toll House Bakery on Route 123 turns out dozens of America's favorite cookies Monday through Thursday every week.

The inn may be gone, but Mrs. Wakefield's original recipe survives. By the way, she dropped each spoonful of dough into a metal ring only ¾ inch in diameter to get one hundred cookies from every batch, but you may want to make your cookies larger.

Toll House Cookies

1 cup butter	2¼ cups sifted flour
¾ cup brown sugar	1 teaspoon salt
¾ cup white sugar	1 cup chopped nuts
2 eggs, beaten	12 ounces (2 cups) semisweet
1 teaspoon baking soda dissolved	chocolate chips
in 1 teaspoon hot water	1 teaspoon vanilla extract

Cream together the butter and sugars. Add the beaten eggs. Add the baking soda dissolved in hot water. Sift together the flour and salt, and add to butter mixture. Stir in nuts, chocolate chips, and vanilla. Chill the dough. Drop by the spoonful onto lightly greased cookie sheets and

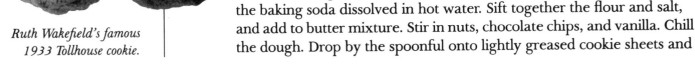

Ruth Wakefield's famous 1933 Tollhouse cookie.

bake at 375° F. for 10 to 12 minutes. Makes 100 small or fewer large cookies.

The Submarines of New London

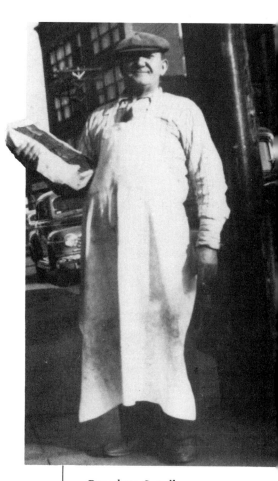

Benedetto Capalbo

It goes by many different names — submarine, torpedo, hero, hoagie, and poor boy to list a few — but the Dagwood-like sandwich beloved by Americans was first called "The Grinder," and it originated in New London, Connecticut, in Benedetto "Benny" Capalbo's grocery.

Benny was a short, stumpy, and slow-moving man who rarely smiled. His attire inevitably consisted of a dark cardigan, a greasy tie, a long white apron, and the same flap cap worn indoors and out. He actually created the sandwich while still living in Salerno, Italy, where he owned a small café. In 1913, he immigrated to America, and by 1920, he had opened his first store.

His grocery, originally located at 18 Shaw Street in the heart of New London's Italian section and later at 367 Bank Street, was the kind of place where customers invariably wandered the aisles, eating a peach and nibbling on cheese while they decided whether or not to make a purchase, literally chewing away at poor Benny's profits.

Benny sold his first grinder in 1926. Properly made, it consisted of salami, provolone cheese, sliced tomatoes, and shredded lettuce, all liberally sprinkled with salt, black pepper, and olive oil. The crucial ingredient was the submarine-shaped loaf of Italian bread. Unglazed and baked for eighteen to twenty minutes in the oven, the bread required that you chew hard, or "grind" away at it, to make progress.

The grinder might have remained a regional anomaly if it hadn't been for World War II. New London was home to a submarine base and a large Coast Guard operation; in all, there were about twelve thousand sailors stationed in the whaling town, and they were particularly fond of Benny's sandwiches. At one time, the submarine base commissary was ordering four hundred to five hundred grinders a day, and Benny employed four women to produce sandwiches. Still, Benny's supply couldn't keep up with demand, and soon other Italian grocers in New London were also in the grinder business. As sailors shipped out to new ports around the country, they would describe for other Italian grocers the sandwich's ingredients. The end result was that the farther away the sailors moved from New London, the further removed from Benny's grinders were the sandwiches they consumed. And the name changed.

91

From the 1890s through the 1920s, Moxie was advertised mainly in newspapers, where sketches reproduced better than photographs. The ads below ran in 1900.

Unfortunately for Benny, he couldn't patent a sandwich, and the good times came to an end with victory in Japan. Sailors were discharged, demand fell, and Benny Capalbo lost his grocery as a result of poor management. When Benny died in 1950, his brief obituary made no mention of his special contribution to American culinary life of the twentieth century.

Just Make It Moxie for Me

There are not many places outside of New England where you can walk into a country store and pull an ice-cold bottle of Moxie out of the cooler. But at one time, Beverage Moxie Nerve Food was the leading soft drink in the country. Invented by a physician in Lowell, Massachusetts, it was quintessential New England, with a bitter, sour flavor that mirrored the taciturn temperament of the native Yankee.

Dr. Augustin Thompson created the drink to capitalize on a thriving private medical practice. The original recipe created in 1876 was a dry compound of gentian root extract, sassafras, and other herbs sold as

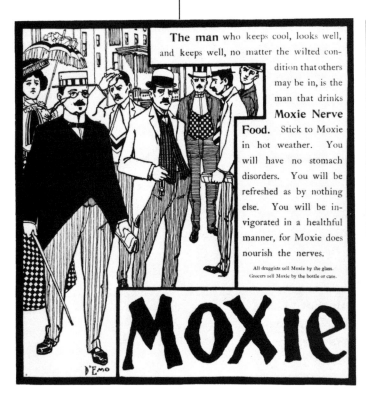

The man who keeps cool, looks well, and keeps well, no matter the wilted condition that others may be in, is the man that drinks **Moxie Nerve Food.** Stick to Moxie in hot weather. You will have no stomach disorders. You will be refreshed as by nothing else. You will be invigorated in a healthful manner, for Moxie does nourish the nerves.

All druggists sell Moxie by the glass.
Grocers sell Moxie by the bottle or case.

A Moxie child is easily recognized. Children who are given **Moxie Nerve Food** are healthy, strong, and happy. The summer heat fails to wear them to a shadow. Moxie fortifies and strengthens the nerves of the little ones as food does their bodies. Children love this temperance beverage.

All druggists sell Moxie by the glass.
Your grocer has Moxie by the case, and will deliver it to your home.

Moxie Nerve Food. As carbonated beverages gained popularity, Thompson added soda water and called it Beverage Moxie Nerve Food, or Moxie for short. The doctor assigned to this concoction the power to relieve "paralysis, softening of the brain, and insanity" along with "brain and nervous exhaustion, loss of manhood, imbecility and helplessness." Who could resist a drink that could restore virility with a single swallow? In the first eight years of production, sales of Moxie rose from five thousand to five hundred thousand dollars.

    Soda water did little to improve the flavor. Though early advertising described it as "a drink to satisfy everyone's taste," even Thompson admitted drinking Moxie was an acquired habit, like smoking pungent cigars. So he boosted sales with a media blitz as audacious as Moxie's name. The Moxie Man, an authoritative figure in a physician's coat, urged the public to "learn to drink Moxie." Cases were delivered to stores in distinctive horse-drawn wagons with storage compartments resembling eight-foot-tall Moxie bottles. With the advent of the horseless carriage, the Moxiemobile replaced the wagons. Where the seat should have been, the vehicle's driver sat astride a life-size aluminum horse; the steering wheel protruded from the horse's neck. There were Moxie fans and Tiffany lampshades bearing the familiar Moxie trademark. There was even a hit song entitled "Just Make It Moxie for Me."

    The public responded enthusiastically. Throughout the 1920s,

Left: A uniformed attendant dispensing Moxie from a Moxie Bottle Wagon parked in front of the Boston Post Office, c. 1890.
Right: The Moxiemobile, with a life-size horse on which the steering wheel was mounted, replaced the horse-drawn carriage.

The Moxie boy was featured on a souvenir handed out at the Boston Food Fair, 1907.

A soldier consuming a tube of packaged rationing through protective clothing.

Moxie was the beverage of choice in most of the country, racking up peak sales of 25 million cases a year and outselling even Coca-Cola.

Eventually sweeter beverages gained favor. By the time the antiseptic Moxie Man was replaced by pretty girls in miniskirts who promised a great new taste, sales had tumbled to a few hundred thousand cases a year. With a yearning for nostalgia, sales in recent years have shown an improvement, but it is a far cry from the days when the country clamored for Moxie and the taste of New England.

Foods of the Future

Imagine cookies made from dry algae. Or cream of algae soup. How about a portion of meat that looks like steak, feels like steak, and maybe even tastes like steak, "engineered" from steer gristle, knuckles, flanks, lips, and heels.

As improbable as it sounds, such ideas have been under development in the Food Engineering Laboratories of the U.S. Army Natick Research and Development Command, in Natick, Massachusetts — the name alone is a mouthful — for the past thirty years. (Service men already dine on "engineered" veal cutlets and are said to prefer them to the real thing.)

"Our intent is not to convert people to eating turkey bars at Thanksgiving instead of whole turkeys," said Dr. Abner Salant, director of the lab. Be that as it may, food created in the Natick lab today may end up in grocery stores tomorrow. Keep your eyes open for the following:

• No-waste steaks, which use up to 72 percent of a steer instead of the present 30 percent in a process known as "flaking." Chunks of meat, gristle, and connective tissue are shaved into tiny flakes, then blended until they fold into each other. Bound with a little salt, the flakes are frozen and extruded into long metal casings. The logs are then compressed and sliced into uniform eight-ounce steaks that look just like New York strip, butt, and rib-eye steaks.

• Pouch food has been touted as the most significant food packaging advance since the metal can. The pouch itself is a three-ply aluminum foil, Mylar package that reduces weight by 40 percent and cuts the amount of energy needed for processing and cooking in half. Inside is a complete, 1.2-pound meal with favorites such as dehydrated peanut butter, crackers, pineapple nut cake, ham and chicken loaf, and strawberries. Home alone after work? Just pop a meal-in-a-pouch into the

ONE POUCH
+
1 CUP WATER
IN
1 BLENDER
=
1 LIQUID MEAL

Left: *What's cooking at your house tonight? The Natick Research Command has developed dental liquids for military personnel unable to eat solid foods. Here we have some delectable strawberry shortcake and (below) some beef stew, chocolate chips, and beef jerky.*

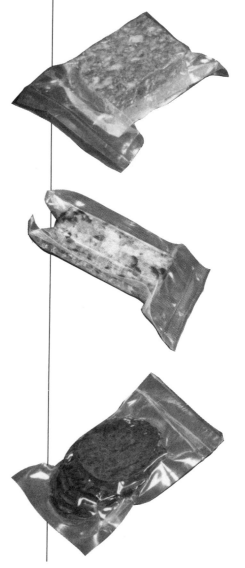

pot and presto. If you are really hungry but too busy to cook, you can warm up the pouch in your armpits.

• Thanks to dental liquids, a broken jaw is no longer an excuse not to eat like a king (or Chester A. Arthur). Culinary delights such as beef burgundy and chicken cacciatore are cooked, frozen, and pulverized, then refrozen in eight-ounce servings. At mealtime, just reheat them in the oven and sip through a straw. Bon appétit!

• Air-dried food is another project expected to return big dividends, especially for those living in small apartments with limited cupboard space. After just three or four hours of drying time, one cabbage can be compressed to a three-inch cube, one-fifteenth the original size. All the fixings for a salad, plus dressing, can be dried and packed into a pouch small enough to fit into a hip pocket.

Ten years from now we may still dine by candlelight, but it may be less for romance than to keep us from seeing what we are eating.

CHAPTER FIVE

Household Helpers

*Making a Difference
In Big Ways & Small*

Father of the Clock Industry

In 1808, Eli Terry, a clock maker working in Plymouth, Connecticut, accepted an order for four thousand wooden wall clocks. Local observers thought Terry had lost his mind. According to conventional wisdom, he would either die before completing the order (he was only thirty-six) or be stuck with more clocks than he could ever hope to sell. What he did instead was father the American clock industry. Over the next thirty years, the clock industry in Litchfield County would grow from a few thousand dollars a year, to well over one million.

Born in East Windsor, Connecticut, in 1772, Terry learned his trade at the feet of masters such as Daniel Burnap. At the age of thirty, he opened his own small shop in Plymouth.

Like all clock makers before him, Terry made wooden wall clocks that were initially hand-crafted, custom-ordered affairs created one at a time. But he had something else in mind. Having heard of Eli Whitney's mass production methods, Terry employed a few men to cut interchangeable wheels and teeth with saws and jackknives. Reporting on this enterprise in *A History of American Manufactures,* J. Leander Bishop wrote, "The manufacture of clocks by water power [by Terry], for a wholesale trade, was . . . regarded by many, as a rash adventure."

But by 1807, Terry was ready to move into a larger mill and commence industrial manufacturing. By one account, in 1808 he began working on five hundred clocks at the same time. That account may be conservative. According to Terry's son, the contract was for a total of four thousand clocks. It was to be the largest order for a mass-produced peacetime product ever, and it marked the beginning of the end for the hand-crafted era. It took Terry three years to adapt Eli Whitney's mass production methods to clock making, but all four thousand clocks were completed and sold.

Having mastered the mass production of clocks, Terry returned to invention. In 1814, he introduced the short clock, or mantel clock. It featured a revolutionary and compact mechanism that relied on the suspension of weights by pulleys on either side of the movement, all housed in an attractive Federal-style case. After several years, Terry sold the rights to his design to Seth Thomas for one thousand dollars, considered a large sum at that time. At first, they both made about six thousand mantel clocks a year, which sold for fifteen dollars each. The clocks proved so popular that production was doubled. By 1825, it was estimated both Terry and Thomas had made more than one hundred thousand dollars on the deal. Eli Terry retired in 1833 a very wealthy man, while his sons,

Eli Terry

brother, and nephew carried on the business in that part of Plymouth known as Terryville.

Howe Invented the Sewing Machine
But Singer Took the Credit

In the 1840s, a young mechanic named Elias Howe, Jr., was working in Boston when he overheard a chance conversation between his boss and another machinist. If he wanted to make some money, Howe's boss advised the other man, he ought to invent a sewing machine that worked. The advice did not fall on deaf ears. Howe quit his job, took out a loan, and set about the task of mimicking the human hand at work. In the process he solved a problem that had befuddled inventors for years — only to have Isaac Singer get all the credit.

Born in 1819 in Massachusetts, Howe left his father's farm and moved to Lowell where he served as an apprentice mechanic in a shop for textile machinery. Like Charles Goodyear before him, Howe had incredible faith in his invention, and incredibly bad luck. With his wife supporting the family from hand sewing, the Howes moved into a shop on his father's farm until that burned to the ground. He then moved into the Cambridge attic of one of his friends.

From studying his wife at work, he finally devised a way to combine the action of two needles on opposite sides of the fabric. At the same time, his machine delivered thread to the fabric from a hole at the bottom of the needle rather than at the top. In 1846, Howe took out patent #4,750 for an "Improvement in Sewing Machines."

Though he believed his hardships were behind him, they were only beginning. Howe introduced the sewing machine with much fanfare, staging a contest in which he outsewed with better quality the efforts of five expert seamstresses. To his disappointment, no tailor was impressed by the results. In 1845, Howe took a job to support his family.

The following year, Howe's brother sailed to England, where a corset maker named William Thomas agreed to buy the machine below cost provided he had the right to duplicate it. Thomas agreed to patent the invention in Elias's name. But once Howe's brother left the country, Thomas patented the device under his own signature. The Brit became the first to show a profit on the sewing machine. When Howe moved his family to London to protect his rights, the corset maker had the audacity

The first sewing machine completed by Elias Howe, Jr. It was this model he took to England, hoping to find manufacturers for it.

to hire him for £3 a week to improve the invention. Desperate for money, Howe sold his British rights for £250 and pawned his American papers in order to send his family back to the States. The Howes' few possessions were lost at sea, and shortly after her return, Mrs. Howe died.

In 1849, Howe worked his way across the Atlantic as a cook, only to discover a booming domestic sewing machine business. He sued Isaac Merritt Singer, the most successful of the bunch, who had also made improvements in Howe's original design. Though the battle dragged on for years, Singer and Howe came to an agreement, and Howe was paid a license fee on his invention. At the age of forty-eight, he died a rich man.

Ebenezer Butterick

Fashion for the Masses

I t was such a simple innovation, but the tissue paper dress pattern was not invented by Ebenezer Butterick until 1863, more than ten years after Howe invented the sewing machine, and Singer made it a household name.

Butterick was born in Sterling, Massachusetts, where his father, a farmer and carpenter, had founded an intellectual discussion group known as the Universalist Society. He learned his trade as an apprentice to a men's tailor in Worcester. At the time of his wedding in 1850, he owned his own business in Fitchburg, where his wife made children's clothing.

At that time, most women made their own clothes by a sort of recycling process, picking apart one worn-out dress to use as a pattern for a new one. Even with Singer's sewing machine, it was a tedious and time-consuming job, and Butterick looked for a way to standardize pattern cutting.

His first efforts involved the children's dresses stitched by his wife. Instead of drawing individual patterns directly on cloth with wax chalk, a standard pattern was cut out of stiff paper which could then be used as a template for one garment after another. Like Eli Whitney's interchangeable muskets, this was assembly-line garment making. Initially, the Buttericks kept the method mostly to themselves, sharing the secret with only a few agents in western Massachusetts. Then in 1863, Butterick gave up his tailoring shop and went into pattern making.

The public reaction was mixed until an unlikely Italian patriot became an overnight hero to thousands of American youngsters. Giuseppe Garibaldi led an army of a thousand Red Shirts to victory in

A 1923 ad for Butterick patterns showed the season's four silhouettes.

Sicily and Naples against the political enemies of King Victor Emmanuel II, and just as Nehru suits were all the rage in the 1960s, every boy in the land wanted to dress like the Italian. The Butterick pattern for the "Garibaldi suit," published on June 16, 1863, sold for fifty cents. It was an immediate best-seller. Three years later, the first women's dress patterns were offered for sale, and by 1868, Butterick had switched to the familiar tissue paper pattern with printed instructions.

Butterick's patterns did more than just simplify dress making for housewives. Like Henry Ford's Model T, which made the automobile affordable for almost all citizens, the Butterick pattern brought fashion within the reach of every woman who had access to a sewing machine, a bit of cloth, and fifty cents for the pattern. When Butterick died in 1903, sales had reached nearly 50 million patterns a year.

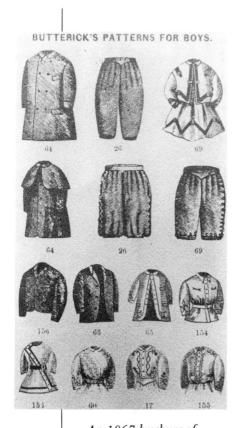

BUTTERICK'S PATTERNS FOR BOYS.

An 1867 brochure of Butterick patterns. The two shirts in the lower left corner are versions of the famous Garibaldi jacket.

Thank the Shakers For the Washing Machine

As everyone knows, cleanliness is next to godliness. To the Shaker communities of New England, scrubbing dirty linens clean was an act of worship.

Of course, no one ever said that worship need be equated with drudgery. In a Shaker village with several hundred families, the one washday a week was potentially a day to test the faith of even the most devout. So in 1858, Brother David Parker of the Canterbury, New Hampshire, Shakers, patented what may have been the first washing machine, "the Wash-Mill." Water and steam both cleaned the clothes and powered the machine. Parker's device was said to be so efficient that the Girard Hotel in Philadelphia laid off fourteen washerwomen after installing a Shaker system. The Sisters said washday was "truly made worship." The Shakers would later come up with a "Centrifugal Wringer," or spin dryer, to further ease work.

By 1876, when an improved version of Parker's machine won a medal at the Philadelphia Centennial Exposition, Shaker washing machines were installed in hotels from the Parker House in Boston to the Tremont in Chicago. The new model was advertised in rhyme:

> Come let us all in love unite,
> And keep our garments clean and white.

At least one New Englander disputes the Shaker claim to the wash-

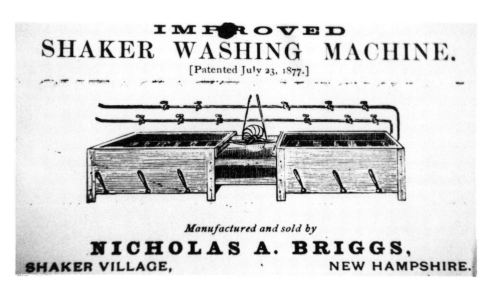

IMPROVED SHAKER WASHING MACHINE.

[Patented July 23, 1877.]

Manufactured and sold by

NICHOLAS A. BRIGGS,

SHAKER VILLAGE, · NEW HAMPSHIRE.

An ad for the Shaker washing machine, patented in 1877.

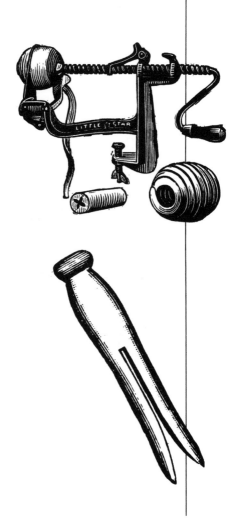

ing machine. Donald W. Hamill, a resident of Chicopee, Massachusetts, claims his great-grandfather, Joseph M. Potter, then of New Britain, Connecticut, was awarded a silver medal by the New Hampshire Agricultural Society for inventing a "Washing and Wringing Machine" in 1860. Unfortunately for Hamill, his great-grandfather never patented his invention, and all that remains of Potter's work is the medal.

What Else Did the Shakers Invent?

Would you believe the common clothespin, a threshing machine, water-repellent cloth, and a wash-and-wear fabric that required no ironing?

In the Shaker communities, idle hands were the devil's playthings, and lest young congregants find their minds wandering to the opposite sex, Mother Ann Lee urged her followers to busy themselves at work.

They were an industrious lot. Along with the washing machine, the Shakers were the first to market seeds in small packets. They also took credit for the flat-sided broom, a metal pen point, cut nails, apple parer and corer, an automatic seed planter, a rotary or disk harrow, the screw propeller, brimstone matches, and a threshing machine.

Whether or not they were actually first with many of these ideas is admittedly difficult to determine. Like poor Hamill's great-grandfather, the Shakers frequently did not patent their inventions in the belief that inspiration derived from God and was not subject to monopoly. But Shaker communities did patent a button for the base of tilting chairs, a

folding pocket stereoscope, and a chimney cap. Our favorite invention
was developed in the Harvard, Massachusetts, community, where Sarah
Babbit, known as Sister Tabitha, had noticed that half the motion of the
pitsaw was wasted. One day, while spinning yarn, she got the idea of
adding a metal disk with teeth to her spindle and created the buzz saw.

How do we explain this remarkable creative outpouring? At least
one social historian has attributed it to chastity: ". . . many younger
members appear to have sublimated their sexual energies, and possibly
their procreative desires, in the only way open to them — by. . . expend-
ing considerable energy and effort to improve the practical arrange-
ments of the 'earthly heavens', " wrote John McKelvie Whitworth in
God's Blueprints: A Sociological Study of Three Utopian Sects.

The Television of Its Day

Long before the first Hollywood director cried, "Action!" the picture-
making capital of the world was the minuscule White Mountain
community of Littleton, New Hampshire. From a four-story brick building on Cottage Street, Ed and Ben Kilburn produced stereographs for
stereopticons by the thousands. With Kilburn cards, the nation witnessed

*From the Kilburns'
Keystone View Company, a
stereoscope of the Great
Sphinx of Giza, Egypt.*

103

the Johnstown flood and the funeral of President William McKinley; they were dazzled by exotic views of foreign lands and amused as a wife shook a finger at her husband with the warning, "I tell you, woman's suffrage would strengthen the solar plexus of the world!" The Kilburns' neighbors were the first American "picture stars."

The stereopticon was invented in 1859 by Oliver Wendell Holmes, the Cambridge, Massachusetts, physician, poet, and essayist. The television of its day, it created a three-dimensional illusion through the use of two lenses, one 2½ inches from the other. Two negatives provided a pair of nearly identical pictures. Mounted in the scope, these twin images were translated by the eyes and mind of the viewer into a single composite scene with depth and perspective. It was like being in the middle of the picture.

The new device created a market for "stereos," sold for twenty-five to fifty cents apiece in stationery shops, bookstores, and by young men working their way through college. That is where the Kilburns came into the picture.

The Keystone View Company was founded in 1866 in a tiny attic studio in downtown Littleton. Ben, known to his friends as B. W., was quick to master the intricacies of stereoscopic picture-making, and his scenes of the White Mountains were an instant hit. Encouraged by success, B. W. traveled the world to bring back pictures of the mysteries of

Stereographs brought the world home. The samples here have the enticing titles of "Glittering Little Figures of the Dance in Siam," "Swahili Women in a Beauty Parlor in Zanzibar," and "Under Full Sail on the Yellow Sea." Typically, the stereographs from the Keystone View Company were accompanied by fairly detailed descriptions.

Mexico, the Holy Land, and Europe. The View Shop was the official photographer of the Colombian World's Fair in Chicago in 1892, and Kilburn cameramen stereoscoped the Klondike gold rush and ladies in bathing costumes on the beach at Atlantic City. More than one hundred thousand scenes were printed. As sales climbed, the brothers created the warped or curved look, an innovation engineered to accentuate the three-dimensional illusion.

Along with travel pictures and news events, the Kilburns featured their neighbors in the first mini-dramas, comedies, and tragedies. Viewers shared the sorrow of a mother at the grave of her child and snickered at the salesman as he fit shoes on the well-formed legs of a lady in a scene titled simply: "Don't Get above Your Business."

The doors on Cottage Street finally closed in 1909 after Ben died. By then, Americans were stuffing their 'scopes and "stereos" into the attic or the trash barrel in favor of newer ideas such as the automobile, do-it-yourself box cameras, and, of course, the moving pictures produced in Hollywood.

Hugh Moore

Paper Cups:
Just What the Doctor Ordered

Most inventors see a need and then design a product to fill it. Hugh Moore, who popularized the Dixie Cup, took a disposable paper cup and convinced the public it was just what the doctor ordered.

Born in Olathe, Kansas, Moore ignored Horace Greeley's advice to move west and came east to seek his fortune, selling advertisements for an agricultural magazine. In 1907, he landed in Boston, where he enrolled at Harvard.

A year earlier, Lawrence Luellan, a Woburn inventor who was also Moore's brother-in-law, designed a porcelain vending machine to dispense five ounces of pure water into a disposable paper cup. The two-piece, flat-bottomed cup he constructed from tablet paper was an afterthought. Moore dropped out of college, and on April 4, 1908, he, Luellan, and a nephew formed the American Water Supply Company of New England in Boston. Vending machines were set up at the transfer points of trolley lines and railroads.

It seemed like the perfect invention. The Anti-Saloon League endorsed the vending machine, claiming that men who wanted nothing more than a drink of water were forced into saloons where they could not

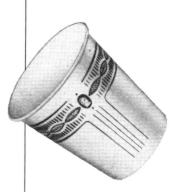

The disposable Dixie Cup that changed America's drinking habits, taken from a 1942 ad.

THE SNOW SHOVEL

Since the first snow in New England may fall any time after Labor Day and is likely to continue right up until Memorial Day, it comes as no surprise that Yankees spend a lot of time thinking about the white stuff. When it comes to getting rid of snow, there are two schools of thought — the philosopher and the utilitarian.

The philosopher is an observer of nature who believes that all things are put on this earth for a reason. Far be it for mortal man to try to divine heavenly purpose. It only follows that if God had intended for man to shovel snow, he would not have created spring, when it all melts away.

The utilitarian believes that God had good intentions but occasionally left a few loose strings that need to be tied up here on earth. Since God has so many other things to do, the utilitarian takes over.

Charles A. Way, of North Charlestown, New Hampshire, was a utilitarian. In 1877, Way added the metal clasp that holds the handle to the snow shovel, proving that where there is a will, there is "A. Way."

When you travel
On one hundred and sixty railroads

YOU will find Dixie cups there for your convenience and protection. Drop a penny in the slot, and presto! Out comes a Dixie—untouched by hands till you take it.

Gone is the rusty dipper that hung at the water cooler, its brim brightened by countless lips. Banished by law and public sentiment!

Just watch the crowd round the Dixie Venders in a great railroad terminal one of these hot summer days, and you will see that they outdraw the ticket windows two to one. Such is the popularity of

DIXIE cups

Round as a glass but white as snow, the very freshness of Dixies invites you to drink.

In public places like railroads, hotels and movies, Dixies are sold; but in thousands of business offices, theatres and soda fountains the management furnishes them without charge for the enjoyment and safety of employees and patrons. Their cost is trifling.

There is a place for Dixies in *your* business and the coupon below is for your convenience.

INDIVIDUAL DRINKING CUP COMPANY INC.
Original Makers of the Paper Cup
220-228 West 19th Street
New York

INDIVIDUAL DRINKING CUP INC. New York.

Gentlemen:—I should like information regarding Dixie service for ....

Name ....

Address ....

Influenza
Sits on the Brim of the Common Drinking Cup

AVOID the common drinking cup as if it were the plague itself. In offices, theatres, stores, on trains—wherever you find it, shun it.

In nearly all states it has already been banished by law. The United States Public Health Commission, Physicians and Boards of Health throughout the country unite in urging the use of individual paper cups.

The dark cloud of an influenza epidemic again threatens. In the name of common prudence it is imperative that you at once install in your home, office, store, or factory the sanitary

DIXIE cups

Insist that they be used in your office. Insist that your children visit only those soda fountains that have them.

The dixie cup is cleanliness personified. It is untouched by human hands until the drinker uses it. Afterward it is destroyed. It is obtained from a dustproof dispenser or vender. It has already proved its worth during years of service.

At this critical time you owe it to yourself to know more about the dixie, and the possibilities of checking the spread of influenza. The coupon below is for your convenience.

INDIVIDUAL DRINKING CUP COMPANY INC.
Original Makers of the Paper Cup
220-228 West 19th Street
New York

INDIVIDUAL DRINKING CUP INC. New York.

Gentlemen:—I should like information regarding Dixie service for ....

Name ....

Address ....

resist the evils of rum. Apparently the temptations were still too much to resist; few bought the water, and the sale of liquor continued unabated.

Moving the company to New York, Moore took a different tack. If no one would buy water, maybe they would buy cups. In December of 1910, with two hundred thousand dollars in financing from W. T. Graham of the American Can Company, the name was changed to the Individual Drinking Cup Company, and a factory was opened on 19th Street. The disposable cups were called Health Kups.

The new company was aided by a stroke of luck. In 1909, Dr. Samuel Crumbine, public health officer for the state of Kansas, launched a successful campaign to ban the communal dipper at public drinking fountains. Not only were fountains affected by the new law, but so was every rail car passing through Kansas. Moore traveled to his home state and convinced Crumbine that his disposable paper cup was the only sane alternative to the dipper. When a Lafayette College professor published the list of viral germs he collected from drinking glasses in a public school system, a sense of urgency swept the country. Moore fueled the fire with promotional material titled "Spare the Children," which depicted a consumptive figure sipping from the public dipper while an infant girl waited her turn. One state after another followed Kansas's lead, and soon practically every Pullman car in the country was equipped with a cup dispenser.

Though Health Kups had caught on, Moore was still not satisfied with the name. It was descriptive, but clumsy. He wanted something that would roll off the tongue. One day in 1919, he happened to notice the sign on a nearby Dixie Dolls factory and liked the way it sounded. Dixie Cup it would be.

In the early 1920s, Moore had another stroke of genius. Ice cream, he realized, was sold only in bulk quantities. So he created a 2½-ounce cup with a flat, pull-up lid that fit into a groove around the rim. He then designed a machine to fill the cups and install the lid. With a ready-made package, Moore convinced the dairies that the public was ready for individual servings of ice cream. This time, he did not even change the name. Dixie Cup became the generic term for a dish of ice cream, just as Kleenex has come to mean tissues.

Dixie Cups were also good for single servings of ice cream. This ad appeared in 1928. Opposite page: Ads from *The Literary* Digest, *1919.*

Cooking by Radio

Percy L. Spencer never had the benefit of a formal education. He learned about life in the woods and machine shops of Maine, where a fellow made the most of the tools at hand. Maybe that is the reason he was the first to think of cooking by radio when the rest of the world just wanted to be entertained.

Spencer grew up poor. After his father died in a mill accident and his mother abandoned the family when he was still an infant, he went to live with his Aunt Minnie, an itinerant weaver. The pair was often without money, and Spencer shot his first deer at the age of twelve to feed himself and his aunt. It was an experience he never forgot. That same year, he quit school to work in a machine shop. Later, a contractor taught him the principles of electricity while they wired a pulp and paper mill.

In 1925, Spencer went to work for the Raytheon Manufacturing Company as a supervisor. The business was based on the Raytheon tube, the vacuum tube that first permitted radios to operate on household AC instead of bulky battery. At that time, Raytheon was locked in a struggle

Amana Radarange microwave oven. When the microwave oven was introduced in the 40s, few imagined how popular this appliance would become.

THE CAN OPENER

The first can opener was patented in 1858 by Ezra J. Warner of Waterbury, Connecticut. With one long blade to pierce the can and a shorter blade to catch on the rim of the container, it looked something like a miniature device for torture, as anyone who had ever missed the can could testify. A hammer and chisel or screwdriver — the tried and true method of can opening since that method of food preservation had been introduced — worked just as well. Only the intervention of the armed forces prevented Warner's device from falling into obscurity. Canned food was popularized in 1861 during the Civil War, and Warner's can opener was standard issue to the Union troops.

Above right: *Amana's first countertop microwave oven, introduced for home use in 1967.*

with RCA for control of the market. The best scientific minds in the lab, with educations from Harvard, MIT, and Tufts, were stumped on how to improve the tube. Spencer passed on a few suggestions he had developed in his spare time to the whiz kids in Cambridge. His innovations kept the company at the forefront of technology at a critical moment, and the boy from Maine left the factory to join the lab.

One day twenty years later, Spencer was working with a magnetron, a vacuum tube that produces extremely short radio waves, or microwaves. When he reached into his pocket for a candy bar, Spencer found that the candy had melted, even though he had felt no heat.

Spencer was not the first to notice the phenomenon. He was, however, the first to find it curious. According to the Raytheon corporate history, he sent out for a bag of "Indian corn" and placed it in front of the wave guide. The kernels popped. The next day, he cut the bottom off a plastic wastebasket and placed an egg inside. When a curious engineer leaned too close, he was splattered as the egg exploded like a kernel of corn. It had cooked from the inside out. Spencer had just invented the microwave oven, or cooking with radio.

Laurence K. Marshall, one of the founders of Raytheon, envisioned a brave new world of centralized commercial kitchens where cooks prepared food almost to completion, then rushed it out to satellite locations where it would be finished off in the new ovens. Immediately he ordered his engineers to design a cabinet for the magnetron with trays inside to heat food. A company contest produced the name "radar range" to describe the new device, but the words were later merged into Radarange.® The first of the new radio ovens was installed in Thompson's Spa restaurant in Boston in 1946. The restaurant is no longer in business.

Reverend Timothy Dwight

A typical Cape Cod house. This full cape is located in Dummerston, Vermont. It was built in 1810.

The House New England Built

The Cape Cod is the house New England gave to America. No other enduring architectural design so reflects the best of Yankee parsimony combined with a secret desire for comfort. Inexpensive to heat, pleasing to the eye, and symmetrical in every way, the Cape reflects, perhaps, the Puritan search for order in nature.

Some authorities maintain the Cape Cod did not originate on the Cape. Those heretics say the Cape is simply a story-and-a-half "early American" which appeared all over New England in the late seventeenth and early eighteenth centuries. Others say the Cape originated in the Plymouth area; but before the canal was built, Plymouth was always, more or less, included as part of Cape Cod.

As far as we know, it was the Reverend Timothy Dwight, president of Yale College, who applied the name, "the Cape Cod House." Dwight arrived in Plymouth in 1800 — before the canal was built — whereupon he recorded for all time that "the houses [there] . . . are generally of the class which may be called with propriety Cape Cod Houses." Reverend

This is a typical three-quarters cape with two windows on one side of the door and one on the other. It is located in Wellfleet, Massachusetts, and was built around the year 1790.

Dwight would not just make up that sort of thing. Besides, in Plymouth stands the oldest example of an original Cape in all of America, the Harlow House, reputedly built in 1677.

We can say with certainty what constitutes a Cape Cod: wood-frame construction, 1½ stories high with pitched roof (optimum range: thirty-seven to forty-two degrees), little or no space between windows and roof gutters, no overhang on the gabled ends, and interiors of small rooms clustered around a central chimney located in line with the front door, thus necessitating, in most cases, walking through one room to reach another. White picket fences, rose bushes, and hollyhocks are optional.

As practical as a pickup truck, the Cape Cod rode out the lashing winds and heavy rains of coastal storms like a sleek schooner on the high seas. The Cape was also the original modular home, with three basic designs to choose from: the half-cape with two windows to the side of the front door, the three-quarters cape with two windows on one side of the door and one on the other, and the full Cape with the door flanked by two windows on either side. Not only modular, but mobile, Cape Cod houses were moved on rollers with horses and floated across the Sound on barges. It was said that the solid Cape could be moved fully furnished; when stoves came into use, the fires were kept burning so cooking could be done along the way.

Commenting on the Cape Cod–style house in 1849, Thoreau wrote, "There were windows for the grown folks, and windows for the children — three or four apiece . . . ." He even knew of one local fellow who cut a window for his cat and a smaller one for his kitten. Eccentric enough to accommodate a cat — that could be the reason the Cape has endured for more than three hundred years.

From Long Houses to Quonset Huts

When the first settlers arrived in what is now Rhode Island, they found the native inhabitants living in houses shaped like cylinders cut in half lengthwise. The natives called them "long houses." They were roomy, versatile structures that were warm in the winter, cool in the summer, and easy to put up and dismantle.

About three hundred years later, in 1941, the U.S. Navy needed some roomy, versatile structures that were warm in the winter, cool in the summer, and easy to put up and dismantle. The navy gave the job of designing such buildings to a team of architects working for the George A. Fuller Construction Company, which was building an air base at Quonset Point. The architects came up with a structure shaped like a cylinder that had been cut in half lengthwise and called it the Quonset hut.

A factory was built in Davisville and in production in nine days. Less than eleven weeks later, the first huts were loaded on a ship headed overseas. More than 32,000 huts were produced at Quonset Point before the job was handed over to Great Lakes Steel Company. By the time the war was over, more than 160,000 huts had been shipped all over the globe. During the first winter of their use, a gale of hurricane proportions smashed into an Allied base in Iceland, sinking ships at anchor and tossing airplanes around like toys. The Quonset huts were undamaged.

At Yale, married students were considered lucky to get half of a Quonset hut during the post-war housing crunch.

Lighter and more capacious than vertical-sided structures, the Quonset huts required less steel to make and took up less room in a cargo ship. The basic hut could be adapted to a host of uses from chapels to barracks to hospitals, but the versatility and utility of the huts were often underappreciated by those who lived in them. "It was like eating Spam," one veteran commented. "Part of the sacrifice you had to make."

When the war was over, returning GIs faced a housing shortage of epic proportions. But the shortage just meant booming business for Great Lakes Steel, which went right on producing Quonset huts for the civilian market. More than 250 styles were offered with a twenty-foot by forty-eight-foot model going for $1,048 C.O.D. Colleges appealed to the government for surplus huts. In one of those huts, at Oregon State University, a young teacher named Bernard Malamud wrote short stories that catapulted him to literary fame. In 1948 a young politician named Gerald Ford ran his first Congressional campaign out of a Quonset hut in Grand Rapids, Michigan. The Killington Ski Area in Vermont opened with a Quonset hut serving as its first base lodge.

When the Korean conflict broke out in 1950, the Quonset hut was recalled to service in the frigid hills and mountains. But back in the States, the housing industry was catching up to the demand. In the prosperity of the Eisenhower years, nobody wanted to live in a Quonset hut any more. The new American dream was a custom-built house.

What was once a booming industry is now mostly a memory, save for seventeen squat steel shells rusting in the salt wind off Narragansett

Gerald Ford's first bid for Congress in 1948 was run out of a Quonset hut.

Bay. These housing dinosaurs have found their place in the National Register of Historic Places, and the versatile Quonset hut now exists mainly as a symbol of the past.

Well, not quite. The New Alchemy Institute, a sort of scientific commune located on Cape Cod, published a report on the ideal "bioshelter," a house of the future that would provide food, recycle wastes, and keep us warm in winter and cool in summer. It looks a lot like a Quonset hut.

"Just Give Me a Home..."

One cold night in 1927, R. Buckminster Fuller found himself alone and depressed in Chicago. He was thirty-two years old, nearly broke, and had just been fired from his job. Drinking heavily, Fuller walked down to the shore of Lake Michigan to end his life.

But "Bucky" Fuller was not the kind of man to undertake anything lightly. Standing on the shore, he came to the conclusion that he had faith in the wisdom of a higher intelligence. "Whether I like it or not," he decided, "I am the caretaker of a vital resource: me!" Fuller resolved from that moment to live for others without worrying about making a living. "If the Intelligence directing the universe really has a use for me," he reasoned, "it will not allow us to starve...."

Born in 1895 in Milton, Massachusetts, Fuller has been dubbed the Leonardo da Vinci of his time. "Officially," he has said with modesty, "I'm a machinist."

After expulsion from Harvard, he began his career as an apprentice in a factory making cotton mill machinery. From there, Fuller devoted himself to a number of projects aimed at deriving the maximum output from minimum material and energy — what he called the Dymaxion principle.

Along with the doomed Dymaxion car he built in the 1930s, Fuller designed a complete, one-piece, die-stamped bathroom that could be installed in a minute, complete with a "fog gun" that shot out a stream of 90 percent air and 10 percent water for more efficient bathing. At the end of World War II, Fuller designed the Dymaxion house, a light-weight, inexpensive structure that could be trucked anywhere in the country for one hundred dollars and erected in sixteen man-days. Both the public and business community responded enthusiastically to Fuller's model home, but after raising ten million dollars in capital, he decided the time was not right for the

R. Buckminster Fuller

Dymaxion house, and dissolved the company. Leading magazines predicted his career and credibility were ruined.

In his own quiet way, Fuller continued experimenting. "The trouble with most buildings," he decided, "is they expend most of their strength just holding themselves up." Fuller found that by stringing together a series of tetrahedrons — four-sided pyramids — in a way that balanced tension struts against compression members, he created a domed structure significantly stronger than the sum of its parts. In math, the shortest distance between two points on a sphere is a geodesic, hence the name. Recalling the Dymaxion debacles, the business community reviewed his plans and collectively shrugged its shoulders.

In 1953, Henry Ford II decided to cover the open courtyard of Ford's Rotunda building in celebration of the company's fiftieth anniversary. Leading architects said it was an impossible task; a dome big enough to cover the courtyard would weigh 160 tons and crush the office building. Fuller took the job. When completed, on time and under bud-

Fuller is holding a Tensegrity Model in his office in Carbondale, Illinois. Tensegrity Theory is based on the principle of the common basic structure of all things in the universe. This principle underlies the theory behind geodesic domes.

get, his dome weighed only 8½ tons. To commemorate the day, he penned a jingle sung to the tune of "Home on the Range":

> Just give me a home in a great circle dome
> Where the stresses and strains are at ease . . .

The geodesic dome was an unqualified success, and for the first time in his life, so was Fuller. A paperboard dome Fuller designed for the marines, dubbed the "Kleenex House," was said to be the first major improvement in military shelter since the tent. Forty-foot-high fiber glass "Radomes" dotted the Arctic landscape along the American Distant Early Warning Line for three thousand miles. The domes withstood winds of up to 220 miles per hour but took only fourteen hours to erect. On the day construction began on a Fuller dome in Hawaii, industrialist Henry Kaiser boarded a plane in California so he could watch the crews at work. By the time he arrived, it was done. Nineteen hours later, the Honolulu Symphony Orchestra gave a full dress concert before an audience of two thousand.

The deity had taken care of Fuller. On January 10, 1964, nearly twenty years after the press had labeled him a charlatan, Fuller was honored as one of the foremost thinkers of his day on the cover of *Time*.

CHAPTER SIX

Striking It Rich

Genius Pays Off

Cyrus Field, a.k.a. Lord Cable

As an eight-year-old boy in Stockbridge, Massachusetts, Cyrus Field was forced to join his smaller brother and sister at their game of making dandelion chains. When he proved inept at fitting one stem into another, young Cyrus was irked by the taunts of the younger children.

"Just wait!" he told them. "Someday I'll make one long enough to go around the world."

Years later, Cyrus Field laid the transatlantic cable on the bottom of the ocean. It was a herculean effort that took thirteen years, $12 million dollars, and sixty ocean crossings. Others might have given up, but Field was an unusually gifted individual. He left home at the age of fifteen with just $8 in his pocket. At the age of thirty-three, he retired from the paper business with $250,000 and a handsome house in Gramercy Park, New York.

But Field was not the kind to sit still. In 1854, Field was introduced to Frederick Gisborne, a lanky Canadian engineer who had tried to lay a telegraph cable from Newfoundland to New York. Gisborne was now broke and wondered if Field would finance the rest of his venture.

Why stop in Newfoundland, Field wondered later, when you were already a third of the way to Ireland? He wrote to Matthew Fontaine Maury, the father of oceanography, and Samuel Morse for advice. Both told him the project was feasible. Encouraged by these two experts, Field formed the New York, Newfoundland, and London Telegraph Company.

Before he could cross the Atlantic, Field needed to link New York to Newfoundland. He bought cable in England, had it shipped to New York, and in midsummer 1855, Field set sail for St. John's. In an omen of what was to come crossing the Atlantic, the expedition ended in disaster not long after it began. In the midst of a storm, the captain cut the cable to save his ship.

While an engineer remained behind to finish the short leg (completed in 1856), Field sailed to England to raise more money for the ocean crossing. The British government agreed to lend steam warships and money to the project, and with their support, Congress reluctantly agreed to join the effort. It took six months to make the twenty-five hundred miles of cable insulated with gutta-percha, but in August of 1857, with much fanfare, a small fleet of ships left Valentia Bay, Ireland.

The cable was far too bulky for a single ship to carry. So the American frigate *Niagara* would carry half the cable halfway across, and the British warship *Agamemnon* would follow with the other half. In mid-ocean, the line would be spliced and then carried on to Trinity Bay

Cyrus Field

117

As the Agamemnon *neared Ireland in 1858, a playful whale swam around the cable as the ship's company watched fearfully.*

in Newfoundland. All went well for 335 miles, until an engineer applied the brakes too sharply to the paying-out machine, and the cable snapped.

Nearly a year passed before a second attempt was made. This time, the ships agreed to convene in mid-ocean; there the ends of the cable would be spliced, and one would sail for Newfoundland while the other headed for Ireland. In June of 1858, Field's work was underway again. This time, they went just three miles before the cable broke. The line was respliced, but when the boats were eighty miles apart, the cable snapped again. After a third failure, the fleet returned to port for more fuel. On July 17, Field once again left the Irish coastline for Trinity Bay. On August 5, 1858, the cable was complete.

The fanfare lasted for three weeks, and Field was the toast of the town. American newspapers dubbed him "Cyrus the Great." An English editorial proclaimed, "The Atlantic Telegraph has half undone the declaration of 1776, and has gone far to make us once again . . . one people." And then the unthinkable happened. While attending a formal reception in his honor in New York, Field was handed a cable from one of his engineers in Trinity Bay. Reading the short note, he suddenly realized the telegram was incomplete: The cable had gone dead. Cyrus the Great was now called a fraud.

Starting over was out of the question. Almost all of Field's fortune had sunk to the bottom with the cable. On top of this came the Civil War and a national depression. Finally, in 1865, two British financiers advanced a large part of the necessary capital, and a cable manufacturer contracted to provide the job at cost in return for shares of stock if the cable worked. The final piece of the puzzle came together when the owners of the *Great Eastern* offered use of the vessel. The ship was a 693-foot, 22,500-ton monster, big enough to carry all of the cable. An engineering masterpiece, it had proved to be a commercial disaster. To recoup some of their losses, the current owners agreed to lay the cable at no charge; if the mission was a success, they would receive $250,000 in cable stock.

On July 23, 1865, with five thousand tons of cable stowed in tanks, the *Great Eastern* headed toward Newfoundland. Only eighty-four miles from shore, the crew detected an electrical fault and began hauling in the cable. Ten miles back, they found a most alarming problem: A two-inch piece of wire had been driven right through the cable. Foul play was suspected, and from then on a guard was posted in the cable tank. (The wire later proved to be a manufacturing defect.)

With only six hundred miles to go, Field was on duty when a flash of silver caught his eye: another shiv in the works. Bitterly, the crew started winding in again. The damaged section reached the top deck, but before the repairs could be made, there came a sound like a pistol shot. The cable snapped and whipped into the ocean. For eleven days the crew scraped the ocean bottom with a five-pronged iron attached to

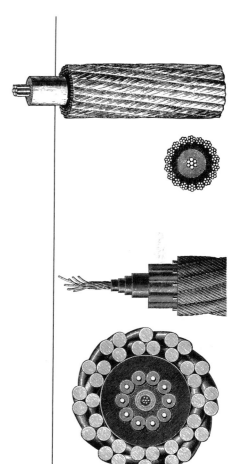

Top: *The cable used on the 1857 and 1858 expeditions is shown on top, with the newer, more heavily protected cable shown on the bottom.*
Left: *The* Agamemnon *and the* Niagara *left from Ireland in 1857, planning to splice together their cables midway. Five days out, an engineer applied the brakes too sharply to the outflowing cable, and the cable snapped.*

several miles of rope to no avail. Once again, Field sailed back to Ireland in defeat.

Surprisingly, England gave him a triumphant welcome. He was known as "Lord Cable," the man who could not be beaten. A new company was formed to raise six hundred thousand pounds of additional capital. A year later, on July 27, 1866, the cable was finally completed on the mainland near Heart's Content, an inlet of Trinity Bay. By mid-August, Field had also retrieved the cable lost on the last journey. After thirteen years, two cables connected the continents. On the first day of operation, the cable brought in five thousand dollars.

Field went on to promote other cables, including one from Hawaii to Asia and Australia. While others looked for their moment in the sun, Field's monument lies mostly underwater, in the proliferation of cables that link every nation on the globe.

Witch of Wall Street

Hetty Green did not have much use for money, though she was one of the richest women in the world. No, for Hetty money was something to get and to have, but not to spend. Born in 1835 to a wealthy New Bedford, Massachusetts, family, she inherited $5 million or so and managed to make it grow by being the most perfect of misers, the Scrooge of Scrooges.

The future "Witch of Wall Street" made her first killing in the booming bonds of the post-Civil War years. At that time she also acquired a millionaire husband, Edward Green, whom she sent packing in 1885 for his spendthrift ways. He died in 1902 with seven dollars and a gold watch to his name.

Green kept their two children on short rations and in secondhand clothes. As a result, Edward lost a leg to gangrene when Hetty balked at paying a doctor; daughter Sylvia was made a nun because convents do not charge room and board.

Her financial dealings were instinctive, brilliant, and preternaturally profitable. She became a familiar figure on Wall Street, striding up and down in a rotting black dress and rubber boots stuffed with millions in cash and securities. She lived in hovels and dined in dives. No economy was too small for Green: She bought newspapers for two cents and resold them for one; she hunted all over town for a misplaced stamp; she once spent hours searching a street for a coin her son had lost.

Her last years were increasingly haunted by fears that somebody would get her money at last. Her banker was trying to poison her, she said; the tax collectors were after her, as were the lawyers or the doctors. She outwitted them all, though; Hetty Green died in 1916 $100 million in the black. The queen of skinflints made her most expensive journey posthumously, when her body was shipped back to Bellows Falls, Vermont, to be buried in the family plot.

Hetty Green in her worn black dress on her daily rounds of the financial district of New York City. Her imposing appearance together with her preternatural understanding of the stock market earned her the title of "Witch of Wall Street."

The Master of Ballyhoo

P. T. Barnum, the master of ballyhoo, was born in Bethel, Connecticut, on July 5, 1810. The P. T. stood for Phineas Taylor, but many of his fellow showmen believed that it stood for "Plenty Tricky."

Barnum began his career as a newspaper editor. Several years later, he was successfully sued for libel, for which he spent sixty days in jail. He sold the paper and moved his wife to New York, where he turned his gifts for exaggeration into a lifelong career.

His start as a showman began in July 1835. Barnum purchased the exhibition rights to Joice Heth, a 161-year-old black woman who once nursed George Washington. At least that is the way she was advertised. As proof, Barnum offered a bill of sale dated 1727, stating that the slave

Right: *Barnum's trained elephants.* Below: *P. T. Barnum and Tom Thumb.*

"Joice Heath" was 54 years old at the time. Though the medical community claimed Heth was a fake, the old woman drew sell-out crowds around New York and New Jersey. She was accompanied by Signor Antonio, a juggler, plate spinner, and stilt walker. When Heth died, Barnum buried her before she could be examined. She was, however, only 80.

As Barnum discovered, no one ever went broke underestimating the innocence of the public. At his American Museum in New York, he exhibited the "Fejee Mermaid," believed to be a preserved mermaid obtained from certain Japanese sailors. Only after Barnum had made handsome profits was it proved the mermaid was a cleverly executed grafting of a monkey with a fish. He made a fortune with General Tom Thumb, "from England" — in reality a five-year-old boy from Bridgeport, Connecticut — who measured less than two feet tall and weighed less than sixteen pounds. His real name was Charles Stratton. In London, Thumb charmed Queen Victoria and starred in a three-act play.

Not all of his productions involved oddities. In 1850, Barnum introduced Jenny Lind, the Swedish Nightingale, to the American stage. But his first love was hype and dazzle, or what he called "The Science of Money Getting and the Philosophy of Humbug." In 1873, he spent a fortune promoting "Barnum's Traveling World's Fair, The Greatest Show on Earth."

Barnum lived in Bridgeport in an Indian-style pavilion that he called Iranistan. It was near a railroad track, and in the field beyond his house, he had an elephant pull a plow for the amusement of the passengers. Near the end of his life, he became partners with Bailey, who

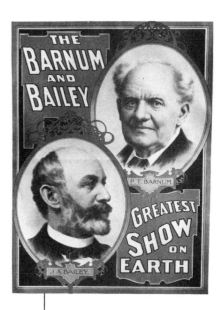

assumed the duties of the circus. The man who made famous the phrase "There's a sucker born every minute" suffered acute congestion of the brain on April 7, 1891. The New York *Evening Sun* ran his obituary early so that he could read it before his death. His estate was worth four million dollars.

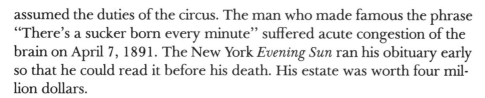

He Froze His Way to Fortune

Clarence Birdseye, a naturalist and writer of books on wildflowers, birds, and mammals, had a natural curiosity about the world around him. "Go around asking a lot of damn fool questions," this native of Gloucester, Massachusetts, liked to say. "Only through curiosity can we discover opportunities, and only by gambling can we take advantage of them." At the end of his life, Birdseye held more than 250 patents for devices as disparate as a recoilless harpoon gun for whaling and a process for converting sugar cane waste into paper pulp. But the one that made "Birds Eye" a household name was the first successful method of fast-freezing food.

In 1912, at the age of twenty-six, Birdseye was working as a fur trader in Labrador when he became interested in the way Eskimos preserved their foods. Back in the States, cold storage was occasionally used to preserve food, but it was a slow process that seemed to rob food of its flavor. Thawed vegetables often turned to mush. Birdseye had an idea

Left: *Iranistan, Barnum's oriental-style villa in Bridgeport, Connecticut.* Right: *The Greatest Show on Earth merged with its chief competitor in 1881 and continued as Barnum and Bailey. This poster is dated 1897.*

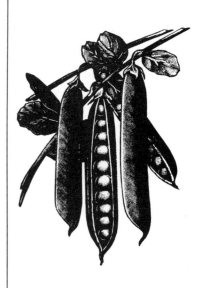

Clarence Birdseye recording data on one of his experiments.

that fast-freezing might seal in freshness.

Birdseye began his experiments with brine, ice, and an electric fan. When he exposed food to a circulating mist of brine at forty-five degrees below zero, the tissue froze so rapidly that damaging ice crystals did not have time to form. Food frozen for months retained its freshness when it was thawed.

In 1923, Birdseye invested everything he owned in Birdseye Seafoods, Inc., and almost went bankrupt in the process. His gamble, however, paid off. In 1929, on the eve of the Depression, the Postum Company bought the rights to his patents and plants for $22 million. Postum was later renamed General Foods. By 1934, Birds Eye accounted for 80 percent of the frozen food business in the country. Twenty years later, frozen foods was a $2 billion-a-year business.

James Ives

Currier & Ives: The National Enquirer *of Their Times*

Working in the age before the camera, Nathaniel Currier and James Ives left a pictorial record of their times that is unequaled. More than seven thousand of their popular scenes were published between 1840 and 1890, and they had distributors in many cities, including London. Though we think of their work as the epitome of Americana,

Currier & Ives were the tabloid publishers of their day, with an unerring nose for the mood of the public. They had as much in common with the grocery store tabloids as they did with Norman Rockwell.

Nathaniel Currier was born in 1813 in Roxbury, Massachusetts. He worked in shops in Boston, where lithography was first established in America, before setting up his own business in New York City at the age of twenty-one. Shortly after his arrival, the city was devastated by a fire that destroyed thirteen acres of downtown property. Four days later Currier was on the scene with a lithograph detailing the event. "Ruins of the Merchants' Exchange N.Y. After the Destructive Conflagration of Dec. 16 & 17, 1835" sold in the thousands and established the Currier name in the city.

Five years later, when the steamboat *Lexington* caught on fire in Long Island Sound, killing more than one hundred people, Currier was on the spot again with a print that included a seven-column description of the blaze. Orders for the *Lexington* were shipped across the country and established for Currier a national reputation.

In 1852, Ives joined the firm as a bookkeeper. The dynamic duo of Americana met through their brothers, who married a pair of sisters. Ironically, neither of them had a serious artistic side. Ives, who had some creative ambition but no desire to starve, is credited with some of the paintings, but no proof exists to substantiate the claim. On occasion,

Nathaniel Currier

An 1868 Currier & Ives print entitled "American Homestead Winter."

Currier and his wife posed for the company artists.

What the pair had was a feel for public taste. Currier & Ives artists covered news events as aggressively as any reporters. Their lurid fires, shipwrecks, and Indian fights were as popular as the sentimental prints of home and hearth. The pair recorded the deathbed scene of every notable person of their day. Pictures were commissioned from various artists, and the black and white prints were hand colored by a dozen or more women in assembly-line fashion. Most of the New England farm scenes were created by George H. Durrie.

Exactly how many prints — priced from fifteen cents to three dollars — were sold is difficult to say; stones for the less popular lithographs were destroyed. One print in the "Darktown Comics" series, however, sold seventy-three thousand copies.

Currier retired from the business in 1880, and Ives was still active when he died suddenly at home in 1895. Their sons succeeded them briefly, but neither Edward Currier nor Chauncey Ives had his father's flair for lithography. Both sons sold their shares of the business. The firm continued to operate until 1907, when the artist's interpretation of the world was supplanted by the realism of photography. When he closed the doors of the business, Daniel W. Logan sold off the lithography stones by the pound.

Visionary or Fraud?

Wallace Nutting

Nearly fifty years after his death, Wallace Nutting is still a controversial figure among historians. With a passion for seventeenth-century furniture, he was one of the earliest historic preservationists. In his Colonial Chain of Picture Houses (of which there were five, one in New Hampshire, three in Massachusetts, and one in Connecticut), tourists could view the colonial ideal. Best known for the hand-painted photographs he sold by the truckload, Nutting created the idealized rural image that most people have of New England today.

And that is the source of the controversy. Though they are popularly accepted by the public as fact, the white painted houses, genteel women, and hooked rugs of Nutting's colonial New England were more a mixture of art and ideal than of historical accuracy.

Contradiction defined him. Nutting could not plane a board, but he directed the manufacture of furniture so exact that experts still have trouble discerning the antique from the reproduction. Wealthy enough to employ a chauffeur, Nutting sat in his office with his hat on and a muf-

fler wrapped around his neck, rather than turn up the heat. He was a New Englander to the core, born in Rockbottom, Massachusetts, and brought up in Industry, Maine.

Until the age of forty-three or so, Nutting preached from pulpits in Maine, Seattle, St. Paul, Newark, and Providence, Rhode Island. When he discovered photography is one of the contradictions of his life. As early as 1900 his work had been featured as center spreads for such magazines as *Country Life* and *Woman's Home Companion.* That said, Nutting wrote in his autobiography that he did not begin to take pictures until after 1901. In search of peace, he took long bicycle rides into the countryside, and on his return, his wife would ask what he had seen. He realized he had been pedaling so furiously that he could not give a report. He then bought a camera and found he had a gift for composition.

In 1904, Nutting suffered a nervous breakdown, resigned from the pulpit, and opened a photography studio near Fifth Avenue in New York City. Little is known about this studio except that he had a saleswoman who traveled throughout the West selling his work. After a year in the city, Nutting and his wife Marietta moved to Southbury, Connecticut, where they lived for six years until they moved to Framingham, Massachusetts, where they remained until Nutting's death in 1941.

In his photography, Nutting favored nostalgic scenes with such titles as "Where Grandma Was Wed." Nutting worked closely with the colorists, who used watercolors to bring life to his black-and-whites. He not only instructed them in the exact shades and tones to use, but also told them they were to paint out telephone poles and cars — twentieth-century intrusions — and blot the sky with cotton balls to give the picture puffy white clouds. He touched a chord, and the photographs sold in the millions.

ISRAEL SACK

He was the first and most esteemed dealer in American antiques. Israel Sack was a Lithuanian cabinetmaker who came to Boston by steamship in 1903. After working for two years as an assistant to an Irish cabinetmaker who repaired furniture and dealt in fakes on the side, he opened an antique shop on Charles Street in 1905.

To stock his shop, Sack made countless excursions into the countryside in search of good old American furniture. By the 1920s, he had branch shops in Marblehead, Massachusetts; New London, Connecticut; and New York City. In 1933, he closed all these shops and consolidated operations in New York City, where his sons still run Israel Sack, Inc.

Henry Ford, Henry DuPont, and John D. Rockefeller all called on Sack to help in broadening their collections, much of which remain today at Winterthur, Colonial Williamsburg, and the Henry Ford Museum.

Wallace Nutting was also a customer of Sack's and nearly sold his collection of Pilgrim furniture to Henry Ford through Sack, but the deal fell through because of Nutting's meddlesome ways.

As his business prospered, Nutting began to collect seventeenth-century colonial furniture, building a collection of more than a thousand pieces, which he sold to J. P. Morgan in 1924 for $140,000; the collection of Pilgrim furniture is now on display at the Atheneum in Hartford. It was a natural step from collecting to making his own line of colonial reproductions and then restoring houses in which to house them. The restorations, such as the Ironmaster's House at the Saugus Iron Works, were a showcase for the Nutting view of colonial America and a vehicle to advertise his furniture.

And that is another of the contradictions of Nutting. To some, he was the P. T. Barnum of the antique world, to others an artist. Whatever his motivation, Nutting looked back to the past and saw the future. He told us how New England should look, and we believed him.

L. L. Bean's Legacy

The creator of the Maine Hunting Shoe was a practical man from Greenwood, Maine, a small town that no longer exists. L. L., short for Leon Leonwood, laid the foundation for a life that combined outdoor living and financial gain at the age of eleven, when his father gave him the choice between a set of steel traps and a visit to the county fair. Bean chose the traps, and that fall he sold five minks for

$1.25 apiece and eight muskrats for a total of $.55.

Between 1893 and 1911, Bean earned his living as a shoe clerk in stores in Yarmouth, Auburn, and Freeport. Along the way, he began to experiment with a more comfortable shoe to wear on hunting trips. One particular combination of leather tops and rubber bottoms appealed to Bean, and he decided to test a pair with a customer at the shoe store. The customer was so enthusiastic that Bean made up one hundred pairs, which he sold for $3.50 each. Unfortunately, the rubber was too light for the stitching to hold, and ninety pairs were returned. Bean refunded the money without a murmur. "Nobody ever won an argument with a customer," he said, instituting a tradition of public good will still in place today.

In spite of the setback, Bean had faith in his shoe. With four hundred dollars borrowed from his brother, he struck a deal in Boston with the United States Rubber Company to make a light rubber sole with a low heel strong enough for attaching to leather tops. Back in Freeport, his wife, another employee, and the local cobbler assembled the boots while Bean put out a three-page catalogue. He was in the mail-order business.

Over the years, Bean built a sportsman's empire on the theory that if he liked it, the public would buy it. By the time of his death in 1967, at the age of ninety-four, the catalogue had expanded to four hundred items, each vouched for by Bean. None would be there, he said, if he would not use it himself with full confidence. On those occasions when a product was returned, Bean sometimes called personally to see how he

Above: *The cover from the 1931 L. L. Bean catalog.* Left: *A glimpse into the sprawling L. L. Bean factory, where the Maine Hunting Shoe is being manufactured.*

Opposite page: *L. L. Bean models the first Maine Safety Hunting Coat.*

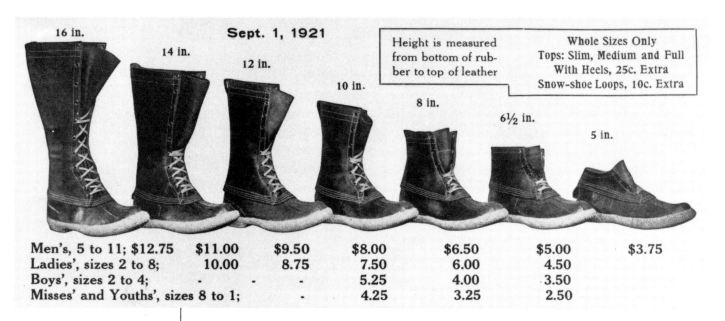

16 in. 14 in. 12 in. 10 in. 8 in. 6½ in. 5 in.

Height is measured from bottom of rubber to top of leather

Whole Sizes Only
Tops: Slim, Medium and Full
With Heels, 25c. Extra
Snow-shoe Loops, 10c. Extra

	16 in.	14 in.	12 in.	10 in.	8 in.	6½ in.	5 in.
Men's, 5 to 11;	$12.75	$11.00	$9.50	$8.00	$6.50	$5.00	$3.75
Ladies', sizes 2 to 8;		10.00	8.75	7.50	6.00	4.50	
Boys', sizes 2 to 4;		-	-	5.25	4.00	3.50	
Misses' and Youths', sizes 8 to 1;			-	4.25	3.25	2.50	

Above: *From the L. L. Bean 1921 catalog, the famous Maine Hunting Shoe is shown in a variety of boot heights and sizes.* Below: *Alfred C. Fuller.*

might improve the product or satisfy the customer — now and again he took a disgruntled buyer on a fishing trip as a gesture of good will. Realizing that you never know at what hour a sportsman may find himself in need of silk long johns, Bean kept his company store open twenty-four hours a day, 365 days a year. While the catalogue today includes selections from twelve thousand different items, ranging from pocket knives to canoe shoes, one of L. L.'s grandsons still approves every item the company offers for sale. The Beans have yet to win an argument with a customer.

Good will may be the real legacy L. L. Bean left behind. When he passed away, Huntley and Brinkley devoted eight minutes of their broadcast to his obituary, and the company received some fifty thousand cards and letters in response.

The Original Fuller Brush Man

Late in his life, Alfred C. Fuller looked back on the company he founded in 1906 and declared that it succeeded in spite of the founder's lack of ability. "There were no highly powered personalities at all, no geniuses in salesmanship or business management," Fuller said. "Our $100 million company is the product of mediocrity since almost everyone who grew up in it was the product of failure who took his job with me in desperation, often despair."

The same could be said of Fuller, who got into the brush business after he was fired from his first three jobs.

He was the eleventh of twelve children born in 1885 on a hard-scrabble farm in Grand Pre, Nova Scotia. At the age of eighteen, Fuller moved to Boston, where his brother and two sisters were living. He tried his hand as a streetcar conductor, gardener and groom, and teamster. In desperation and despair, he finally took a job with the Somerville Brush and Mop Company selling brushes door to door.

By 1906, he had managed to save $375.00 and decided to go into the brush business for himself. In his sister's basement he set up a $15.00 brush-making machine and a $3.75 lamp, an extravagance his sister claimed could lead to ruin. At night he manufactured a line of twisted-in-wire brushes which he then peddled door to door. Originally, he produced just seven models — scrub, bath, clothes, bottle, hand, floor, and radiator.

Devoid of a salesman's personality, Fuller made politeness the point of his spiel. "Good morning, madam," he would begin, "if there is anything wrong in your house that a good brush could fix, perhaps I could help you."

Perhaps he could. On his first day, Fuller sold six dollars worth of brushes. By 1910, when he rented a shed in Hartford for eleven dollars a month, he employed twenty-five salesmen and six workers. By 1937, the Fuller Brush Company was selling $10 million worth of brushes a year. Eventually, the line expanded to more than 125 brushes, household cleaning items, and women's cosmetics, sold by a bevy of "Fullerettes."

Women made a brief appearance as saleswomen for Fuller Brush between 1945 and 1947. Resentment from the full-time male salesmen forced Fuller to fire all the "Fullerettes," as they were known. In 1965, competition from Avon led Fuller to reconsider, and women once again sold the Fuller Brush line.

The Fuller Brush Man was an icon of the American scene. So familiar was he that the Big Bad Wolf masqueraded as a Fuller Brush Man to trick the unsuspecting Three Little Pigs in the Walt Disney movie. At one time, it was estimated that Fuller's army delivered their wares to eighty-five out of every one hundred American homes. In Alaska, they delivered by dog team.

By the early 1970s, when the Fuller Brush Company was bought out by Consolidated Foods, there were twenty-five thousand Fuller Brush persons and sales of $130 million a year. Over the years, it was

"Nowhere can dust or dirt escape the absorbing strands of the Fuller Mops" boasted this 1922 ad from The Saturday Evening Post.

estimated that twenty-five million "Handy Brushes" had been given away.

Looking back on his long career, Fuller said simplicity was the secret of his success. "We who . . . aspire to little may have something to tell the world, since there are so many of us," he said. "In our lives there may be lessons of value to those of greater genius, if they would heed us briefly. Perhaps we think more clearly than minds more complicated."

Ham Inventor & Yankee Trader

Earl Tupper often described himself as just a "ham inventor and a Yankee trader." If that is the case, then Marilyn Monroe was just another blonde. Tupper's pliant plastic containers created a household revolution.

Born in 1907 in Berlin, New Hampshire, Tupper first displayed a knack for business when as a farm boy in Harvard, Massachusetts, he discovered he could make more money with a lot less work by buying and selling other kids' vegetables than by raising his own. In the 1930s, while working as a

Above: *Its incredible practicality insured Tupperware's success.* Right: *Earl Tupper, chemist by trade, entrepreneur at heart.*

chemist for DuPont, Tupper founded a mail-order business to sell combinations of combs, toothbrushes, and other toiletry items. By 1937, he had made enough money to leave DuPont.

Out on his own, he set to work with polyethylene, a new synthetic polymer that produced a soft, durable plastic. There were already plastic household items on the market, but they were heavy, rigid, and easily broken. Tupper came up with a method to make polyethylene tough enough to withstand almost anything except knife cuts and boiling water. At the same time, his new plastic had incredible resiliency. He dubbed the new material "Poly T," claiming "there have been too many bum articles called plastic." He then invented the molding machines to press Poly T into twenty-five household items ranging from poker chips to ice cube trays.

In 1942, he formed the Tupperware Corporation at Farnumsville, Massachusetts, of which he was the president, general manager, and sole stockholder. But before he had a chance to produce anything, World War II intervened. Three years would pass before Tupper introduced his first product, a seven-ounce bathroom tumbler. It was followed a year later by the same glass in pastel shades.

The following year, Tupper introduced his incredible plastic bowls with the airtight seal. Selling for about thirty-nine cents each, Tupperware stunned the public. The American Thermos Bottle Company or-

dered seven million nesting cups from Tupper. The Museum of Modern Art wanted one of his bowls to be included in a show of useful objects. A Bay State insane asylum found Tupperware to be an almost ideal replacement for noisy aluminum cups and plates. By 1947, sales had reached $5 million annually.

Ever the Yankee trader at heart, Tupper saw that Tupperware sold best through the party plan, a system whereby housewives would invite their friends, neighbors, and relatives to their homes for a party. There would be games, followed by refreshments and a Tupperware demonstration. For her time and trouble the hostess would be paid — in Tupperware. It sure beat the high cost of advertising.

In 1951, Tupperware Home Parties was incorporated, and retail sales were discontinued. Within three years, Tupper had signed up nine thousand dealers who arranged parties, and sales had topped $25 million.

In 1958, Tupper sold his company to Rexall Drugs for more than $9 million and faded from public life. The "ham inventor and Yankee trader" had just completed his best swap yet. He died in 1983 in San José, California.

Perhaps the key to Tupper's unprecedented success was the Tupperware party. Women invited their friends to their homes for an evening of games, refreshments, and, of course, a Tupperware demonstration. This photograph was taken at a typical Tupperware party in the 1950s.

135

CHAPTER SEVEN

Dreams That Failed

Or How Genius Is Part Luck, Part Inspiration

Mark Twain's Incredible Nightmare

At the end of the year 1880, Samuel L. Clemens, known the world over as Mark Twain, was, by the uninflated standards of that day, more than comfortably affluent. *Innocents Abroad, Roughing It,* and *Tom Sawyer* had all sold well, and the recently completed *Prince and the Pauper* was not expected to break the pattern.

In his peaceful life of prosperity there was but one tiny ripple: a small investment in a mechanical typesetter under development by a James W. Paige at the Colt arms factory.

Part genius, part visionary, Paige was a small, neat, dapper man equipped with the smooth tongue and persuasive manner of a confidence man, and some of the relaxed morality of one, too.

The machine Paige was developing set and distributed type at the rate of three thousand ems per hour — three times faster than a human operator. Upon witnessing this, Twain added three thousand dollars to his original investment of two thousand dollars, which Paige applied to several improvements he had in mind. For several years, work on the typesetter proceeded with much experimentation and many stoppages. Every now and then it became necessary to put in additional money to keep things moving.

Twain had already invested a total of about thirteen thousand dollars when Paige offered Twain a half interest if he would provide the capital to complete the typesetter. Paige assured Twain that twenty thousand dollars would be ample, but to be on the safe side perhaps they should allow thirty thousand. At the time, the typesetter was capable of between thirty-five hundred and four thousand ems an hour. Any inventor but Paige would have put it on the market then and there, and any promoter but Mark Twain would have made him do it.

But Paige was a slave to his own creativity. The machine required an assistant to "justify" the lines of type — that is, make them the same length. Paige was determined to do the justifying automatically. Twain, enamored of the typesetter's complexities, readily agreed.

Eventually, Twain's thirty thousand dollars ran out with the machine still unfinished. The smooth-talking inventor assured Twain that four thousand dollars would see them through. Twain was in a trap. Before long this money ran out, and Paige was back for more.

Now began a sort of fantastic snake dance with the typesetter consuming three thousand dollars a month, the completion date always promised within a few weeks and forever receding like a mirage. By early 1888, Twain had put in eighty thousand and Paige was promising

Mark Twain

the machine would be ready by April. When April arrived, the completion date was moved to September, and so it went.

Finally, on January 5, 1889, the Paige compositor was completed — and it worked! It set, spaced, and justified type automatically and at a tremendous speed. It was all they had dreamed it to be.

Surely the machine was now ready for the market? Paige said no, not *just* yet. There were still two or three improvements to be made, minor things, a matter of a few days only.

Twain, as always, reluctantly agreed. Expenses rose to four thousand dollars a month. *A Connecticut Yankee* was published and did well, but all the profits went into the typesetter's capacious maw. Twain was forced to borrow money.

The year 1890 was a nightmare. Twain did little or no literary work. All his energies were spent in trying desperately to interest outside capital in the typesetter.

Finally, millionaire Senator J. P. Jones of Nevada declared that if the machine really operated as well as Twain said it did, he was prepared to put in one hundred thousand dollars and head up a group to promote the Paige typesetter on a nationwide basis.

Paige assured Twain the machine was complete and ready to demonstrate. On the appointed day Jones and his coterie proceeded to the factory to discover the inventor had decided to add an air blast to the machine and miscalculated the time required for the job. The typesetter was lying on the floor completely disassembled.

Jones and his party left Hartford on the next train.

In 1891, there was a stock market crash followed by a business recession. Twain's affairs, already bad, grew worse, and he became seriously depressed. Neither Twain nor his beloved wife Livy was in the best of health, and a tragedy might have ensued save for the help of a Standard Oil capitalist named H. H. Rogers.

Rogers was one of the tough old breed of financiers who flourished in the days before the trusts were broken up. Rogers became Twain's business adviser and addressed himself to untangling the confusion of typesetter royalties and options, which by now involved many investors. When it was eventually straightened out, Paige was induced to sign a new contract.

The situation of Twain's publishing house, the Charles L. Webster Company, was hopeless, and in April 1894, the firm went into bankruptcy. Rogers steered this through successfully, the creditors getting fifty cents on the dollar. Mark Twain promised that he would someday pay each creditor in full, but no one believed it.

There was still hope for the typesetter. The *Chicago Times-Herald* agreed to give it a trial; should this turn out successfully, the millions might yet pour in.

The Paige compositor was installed and worked magnificently —

Above: *An early edition of* Tom Sawyer *by Mark Twain. Proceeds from this best-seller, as well as from several others, were sunk into Paige's typesetter.*
Left: *Patent drawing of the Paige typesetter, 1895.*

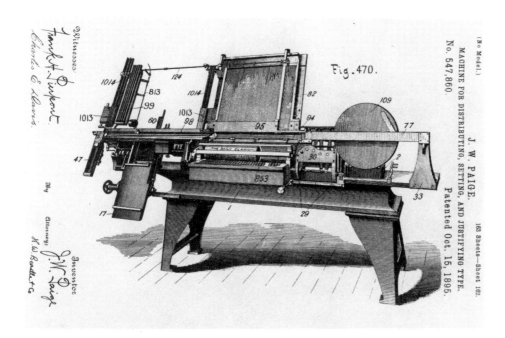

for a time. It set type at a phenomenal rate. But it was *too* complicated; it got out of adjustment easily, and then Paige himself had to be sent for, as no one else really understood the intricate mechanism.

No doubt regretfully, the *Times-Herald* threw it out. It never received another chance. The patent was awarded in 1895, but by that time, it made little difference.

Only two models of the Paige typesetting machine were ever built. One went in a scrap-metal drive during World War II. The other is on exhibition at the Mark Twain Memorial in Hartford.

The machine is worth study. Nine feet long and weighing more than three tons, it was operated by a one-twelfth horsepower steam engine. It had eighteen thousand separate parts, not counting springs, cams, and bearings. The keyboard had 109 characters. Its rate of composition — twelve thousand ems per hour — was not equaled for fifty years!

The patent required 204 separate drawings, which cost two thousand dollars. The patent attorney got ten thousand dollars more.

From first to last, the Paige typesetter machine cost about $2.3 million. Mark Twain, the heaviest single investor, lost $190,000.

Most of us are familiar with Mark Twain's long and courageous fight to recoup. He wrote, embarked on an exhausting worldwide lecture tour, and drove himself without pity. In January 1898, at the age of sixty-two, he had accumulated enough to pay off every creditor one hundred cents to the dollar.

Mark Twain's home in Hartford, Connecticut.

The Paige typesetter had, of course, taught Mark Twain a bitter lesson.

Of course. Yet within *one month* of settling his debts, he was negotiating for the rights to a marvelous machine that designed carpet patterns, planning to organize a company to lease the machines to the carpet factories of the world and make millions.

It was not to be. He wrote enthusiastically of his plan to H. H. Rogers, who still acted as his business adviser. Rogers turned down the scheme cold, doubtless with a deep sigh and a weary shake of his head.

Steam into Melody

Chances are good that you have never heard of Joshua Stoddard, but if you have ever been to an old-fashioned circus, you have probably heard from him. The inventor of the steam organ was a Vermonter from the town of Pawlet who conceived the notion of turning steam into something melodious while living in Worcester, Massachusetts. He dreamed of an instrument for worship, a substitute for church bells. When he received his patent in 1855, Stoddard blessed his newborn baby with a name as lofty as his ambition: "Calliope," the Greek muse of eloquence and epic poetry. What he came up with is the most indefatigably strident and the most wondrously loud part of the circus.

There was nothing quite like the steam organ. It had a boiler fired either by wood or coal. Firm pressure on a key opened a valve that sent the steam coursing into a pitched pipe. Undeniably a definite and determined sound was produced; whether or not it was music of the gods was a matter of opinion. There were those who laughed at the presumptuousness of equating this eight-key steam boiler with the land of Odysseus, and those who laughed even harder when someone sat down to play it. The critics dubbed it "Stoddard's Madness." But Stoddard had a stiff backbone; the louder the criticism, the louder he played.

It did require a Calvinist fortitude to play the calliope, and not just to withstand the flat-out derision of audiences. Pressing the hot brass keys blistered fingers and sent a spray of steam, a shower of sparks, and a blast of sound into the air. "Deafness was said to be an occupational hazard of it," the National Geographic Society once commented, "and drunkenness the only palliative."

Stoddard carried on. He organized the American Steam Music

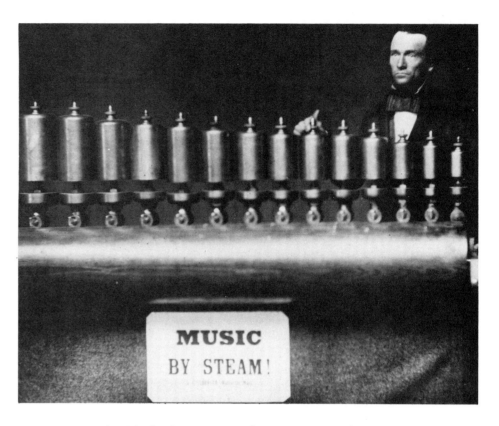

Joshua Stoddard and his calliope.

Company, and with the legitimacy of incorporation behind him, he hoisted his invention on a flatcar and embarked on an impromptu whistle-stop concert tour. The climax was reached on the Worcester Common on July 4, 1856, when Stoddard's sister played patriotic airs on the calliope while Stoddard stoked the boiler.

In spite of his efforts, the church was not seduced by the charms of an instrument with hell fire in its belly. Instead, a Hudson River steamer, the *Glen Cove,* installed the first calliope, calling passengers aboard for river cruises. When P. T. Barnum mounted a calliope on a gaudy red and gold wagon pulled by eight matched Percherons, its secular use was determined for all time. "Calliope," the circus posters ballyhooed. "The wonderful Operonicon or steam car of the muses!"

Samuel Cabot

Too Warm for the North Pole!

Samuel Cabot enjoyed a naive belief that everything in the world had been put there by a benevolent deity for some useful purpose. When he came upon some material for which there was no apparent use, he tried to second-guess the deity's intentions by discovering a use for it.

Eelgrass was such a material. In Chatham, at the elbow of Cape Cod, where the Cabots summered, eelgrass piled up in great rolls on the sands at the high-tide mark. Cape natives had no use for it; it made an ugly mess on the beach and was just a plain nuisance. That was just the kind of challenge that appealed to Cabot.

His eelgrass investigations started in the summer of 1893. After learning that early settlers along the coast kept their houses warm by stuffing eelgrass into the walls, Cabot filled several large pits on his land in Chatham with eelgrass and mounted thermometers at strategic locations in and around them. From the temperature readings, he became convinced that conveniently packaged eelgrass installed by a carpenter would make efficient house insulation. A machine was installed at the Cabot factory in Chelsea to stitch layers of the grass between two sheets of heavy kraft paper, forming long strips of insulation thirty-six inches wide and up to an inch thick. The material was known as "Cabot's Quilt."

Well liked by architects and builders in the cold North, Cabot's Quilt received a real boost when it was installed in the headquarters of the Scott South Polar Expedition of 1911. Arctic explorer Donald B. MacMillan also used eelgrass insulation at his camp in North Greenland. "That Cabot Sheathing is wonderful stuff . . ." he wrote to the company. "We have never been cold, but many times too warm and obliged to

Above: *Cabot's Quilt came in three different widths: single, double, and triple ply.* Below: *Trucks loaded with eelgrass destined for Cabot's Quilts, unloading at a Cabot warehouse in Nova Scotia.*

Left: *A weather station insulated with eelgrass on top of Mount Washington.* Right: *The cozy and warm living quarters of the weather station.*

throw open the doors."

Too warm on the North Pole! Cabot could not buy that kind of advertising. Although it never moved in great volume, Cabot sold enough of his quilts to keep two machines running eight hours a day. He had become so good at making something out of nothing that the company acquired a lot of coastal real estate in Yarmouth County, Nova Scotia, where eelgrass piled up on the beaches in windrows six feet high. Cabot had divined the mind of the deity.

Then again, the deity works in strange and mysterious ways. Beginning in the 1930s, Cabot began to notice an ominous trend: There was much less eelgrass. A blight had infected the coastal grass, and shipments dipped from twelve hundred tons of grass a year to eight hundred, then three hundred, one hundred, and finally the harvesters gave up. For a time, Cabot imported eelgrass at twice the previous price from Germany, but World War II put a stop to that. By the time the blight finally abated in the late 1940s, the market had found other insulation materials, and the quilt machines had been dismantled.

He Died in the Saddle

In his time, Sylvester H. Roper, the son of a farmer from Francestown, New Hampshire, patented many useful devices. The steam-powered bicycle is not one of them, but it is the invention for which he will be remembered best.

Like Elias Howe, Roper learned the machinist's trade in Boston. Before Howe invented the sewing machine, Roper was already famous for developing one of the first practical knitting machines used in the region. He went on to create the hot air furnace. As early as 1869, he had equipped a heavy two-wheeled velocipede with a steam engine and used it for a decade.

Roper introduced his last invention in dramatic fashion on June 2, 1896. He was then a seventy-three-year-old man, and bicycle racing was all the rage. That afternoon, he lined up with a group of racers less than half his age at Boston's Charles River bicycle track.

Despite catcalls from the racers and laughter from the judges, Roper was allowed to enter. The old man pushed his bike, powered by an eight-horsepower engine, onto the track and invited the others to follow. When they agreed to humor him, Roper reached into a sack and extracted a handful of coal to fire the tiny furnace. They were off.

At first, the steam bike trailed far behind the pack. But as the pressure in the boiler rose to 180 pounds, about that used later in locomotives, the little engine perked up. One by one the wheelmen dropped out of the race, as Roper lapped the other bikers three times. Finally, only the old man and his steam bike were left on the track. Roper opened the throttle and circled the track in a record time of 2 minutes, 1-2/5 seconds. It was his last lap. With the bike howling along at forty miles per hour, spectators noticed the front wheel begin to wobble. Seconds later Roper veered off the track and onto the sand.

A crowd rushed to where the inventor lay. When they picked him up, it appeared as if he had only a slight cut above the temple. A medical examination later revealed that Roper had died of a heart attack before his wheel hit the dust. "Died in the Saddle" read the headline in the *Boston Daily Globe*. Amazingly, Roper had had the foresight to shut off the steam boiler before he crashed.

A reproduction from The Boston Daily Globe, *June 2, 1896.*

The Monorail Train Came Too Early

As sightseeing attractions go, the gritty yards of the Portland Company, a builder of steam locomotives, were not highly rated. But on one particular day in 1889, the better part of the citizenry of Portland, Maine, crowded the yards to get a look at the Boynton bicycle monorail locomotive.

The monorail was the brain child of a persevering and rather humorless man named E. Moody Boynton. In the 1880s, he began to stir

public interest with his outspoken comments about American railroads. Fast, lightweight trains, he stoutly maintained, would cost less to build and operate and would encourage the railroads to expand and improve their service. Viewed with the hindsight of history, he probably was right.

His creation included a single eight-foot driving wheel slung between two parallel boilers just ahead of a two-story cab. Cylinders and main rods mounted beneath the smoke box and boiler drove the single driver along a single running rail, while a guiding rail overhead, supported by arches, steadied the engine. Boynton's engine was built at the Portland Company's works only after a Newburyport shop threw up its hands and quit. An old-line manufacturer as staid as Boynton, the company tackled the engine gingerly in a triumph of curiosity over skepticism.

In one respect, the monorail was an immediate success: It drew crowds to witness the trial run along a short stretch of specially built track. Boynton rode in the second-story cab, wearing a fur hat and look-

Photo of the monorail taken from the yard of the Portland Company. Note how the train is suspended from the cable. It is this crucial support that enabled the train to travel along a monorail.

146

Locomotive No. 1 of the Boynton Bicycle Railway Company, taken in the yards of the Portland Company, Portland, Maine.

ing more like a minister than an inventor, according to one witness. And in one respect it worked: The engine ran. After the demonstration, Boynton optimistically told the press that his engine would pull four cars carrying eighty-eight passengers each at the unheard of speed of one hundred miles an hour. He spun out a fantasy of skinny cars and their skinnier track threading their way through inaccessible gorges and over tall mountains.

Fantasy is all he ever created. Longer, heavier trains became the fashion, and Boynton refused to acknowledge the major objection to his system: His engines and cars were not interchangeable with conventional rolling stock. For years, Boynton sought and was denied legislative permission to build his monorail. He died a disappointed man who never lived to see the lightweight trains that now embody his beliefs go into service.

Douglas Fairbanks, Sr.

The Charming, Seductive Wasp

She was from a small town in Vermont, seductive, and maybe a little capricious, and in 1920, Douglas Fairbanks fell in love with her at first sight. What captivated the movie star's fancy was the Wasp, and for certain charms there was never another motorcar like her.

When Karl Hamlen Martin formed the Martin-Wasp Corporation in 1919, he catered to the motoring enthusiast who wanted something completely different from any other offering on automobile row and who had sufficient coin to indulge such whimsy. The

Karl Hamlen Martin

Right: *Peter Hekk, the famous automotive illustrator, drew this picture of the Wasp for the cover of a book by his friend Kevin Marvin, the foremost authority on the Wasp. For the license number of the car, he chose the dates of Marvin's wedding.*

thirty-year-old creator of the beauty from Bennington equipped every model with a St. Christopher medal, and he made it clear that no Wasp would be sold without this feature.

She was flashy in design without eccentricity. The fenders were pointed, the front ones projecting straight forward rather than curving as on conventional motorcars of the period. Across the radiator was a diagonal metal strip that, as it unhappily turned out, interfered with successful cooling. Special parking lights were fused through the glass of the windshield. The Wasp had an aluminum body over a wood frame, all trimmed in seasoned white ash. Between 1920 and late 1923, an estimated thirteen cars were built and marketed at prices ranging from five thousand to six thousand dollars.

The car was initially exhibited in conjunction with the New York Auto Show in January 1920. Martin did not complete his first Wasp until two weeks before the opening of the show, and so he hadn't been able to reserve space for it at the Grand Central Palace. Instead he arranged to display the Wasp in the main lobby of the newly opened Hotel Commodore. Stepping out of the elevator, Douglas Fairbanks, Sr., bought the car on the spot and shipped it to Hollywood.

So exclusive was the Wasp that Martin was convinced that free advertising was all that was needed to promote his product. Instead of buying paid ads, Martin submitted sketches of elegant designs on the

Wasp chassis to magazines such as *Vogue,* which published them. One Mrs. Outhwaite purchased the only Wasp sold locally, and when Martin needed a picture, he photographed the Outhwaite vehicle in a local setting.

Exclusivity proved to be the Wasp's demise. Martin could never build many of them. A longer model with a larger engine was late leaving the drawing board and didn't appear until 1924. Priced at ten thousand dollars, the new Wasp was the most expensive domestic car of its time, with the exception of the American Rolls Royce. Two of them sold. In mid-1924, work commenced on a third chassis for a gentleman in Atlanta, but the potential buyer died before the car was completed, and the order was canceled. The company was soon out of business. Martin briefly drove the final car as his personal transportation around Bennington. In 1953, he sold it to Henry Marvin Dodge, an Ohio-based car connoisseur, who spent seven years restoring it. Dodge presented the Wasp to the Bennington Museum in 1982; it is now on permanent display in its own gallery.

Top: *Karl Martin and Mrs. Outhwaite out for a cruise in one of the few Wasps ever built.* Bottom: *A bronze St. Christopher medal was built into every car.*

The Dymaxion Car

When she was twenty years old, Nannie Dale married Edward M. Biddle. The Dales and Biddles were of the Social Register set, but Nannie found all that as thrilling as stale ginger ale. During the winter of

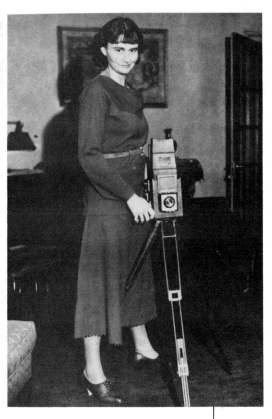

Nannie Dale Biddle

The Dymaxion car from a drawing by Buckminster Fuller.

1932, she shared an isolated cabin with a trapper and his wife in the interior of Alaska, without Mr. Biddle. Upon her return that spring, she made plans for a gold-prospecting expedition, a scheme she mentioned to her old friend, R. Buckminster Fuller.

Today, Fuller is world famous as the architect of the geodesic dome. In 1932, he was just getting started. Listening to Nannie's plans, Fuller glared at her through his thick spectacles. "Why not do something useful with your money?" he challenged. "Turn it over to me and I'll revolutionize the automotive industry."

Fuller had designed a three-wheeled automobile called the Dymaxion; the word was a copyrighted combination of dynamic, maximum, and ion. When Nannie agreed to put up the cash, Fuller suggested they hire W. Starling Burgess, a poet, mathematician, and naval architect, to help complete the car. Burgess's specialty was the design of fast sailing vessels, such as the 1930 America's Cup defender *Enterprise*.

Since 1932 was the nadir of the great Depression, people with the money to buy yachts were scarce. Burgess jumped at the opportunity. In January of 1933, the 4 D Company was formed (it stood for Fourth Dimension), and the pair rented a defunct auto factory in Bridgeport, Connecticut. Work on the prototype was begun in March and ready for the test track that July.

When it was unveiled, the Dymaxion I was one of the most amazing cars ever built. A nineteen-foot-long cylinder encased in an aluminum skin, it looked like a frankfurter on three wheels. The single wheel in the

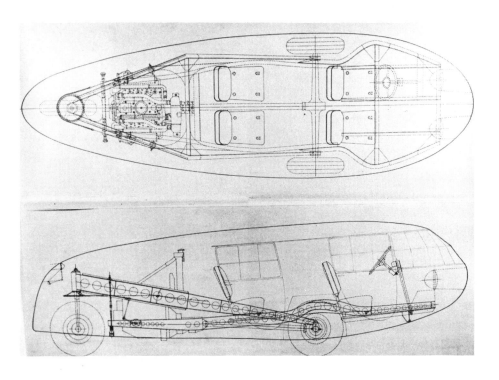

back did all the steering and could pivot ninety degrees. The windows were of shatterproof aircraft glass. There were rearview periscopes for both front and rear seats and room for eleven people. Traveling at an average speed of 70 miles an hour, it got 40 miles to the gallon of gas. Top speed was 120. It looked like the car of the future, and it never went into production.

Neither Fuller nor Burgess had any interest in becoming auto magnates. Nannie just wanted to get her money back with a little profit. They agreed to build a few more cars (in all, three were manufactured) and then arrange for some large firm to buy them out. The deal looked set when a British syndicate sent engineering expert Colonel W. F. Forbes-Sempill to test the car.

Then fate intervened. The car was delivered for testing in Chicago by a racing car driver named Turner. The Dymaxion I handled like a dream, and at the conclusion of the tests, Turner offered to drive the British engineer back to the airport. While the Dymaxion was stopped at a red light, a car owned by a Chicago politician pulled up alongside. Challenges were made, and when the lights changed to green, the cars went careening through the streets. The driver of the politician's car lost control and crashed into the Dymaxion, rolling it over several times. Turner was killed instantly, and Forbes-Sempill was seriously injured.

The next day, coast to coast headlines such as "Three-Wheeled Car in Disaster" emphasized the unusual design of the Dymaxion. The syndicate lost interest, and no American manufacturer was willing to put an unorthodox car with a bad reputation into production.

There was a happy ending to the story, however. Fuller, of course, went on to gain worldwide fame; Burgess designed, among other things, two more successful Cup defenders. And though Nannie lost her investment money, she finally divorced Edward Biddle and married Burgess.

Almost the Father of Flight

Rufus Porter

Back before the Wright Brothers were even born, Rufus Porter designed the first airliner, a one-hundred-passenger flying craft that never evolved beyond the design stage. Had he ever gotten his craft off the ground, we might be honoring Rufus Porter as the father of flight instead of the Wrights. Today, Porter's treatise on flight is all that remains as one of the footnotes of aviation history.

That Porter's ideas never achieved fruition comes as no surprise, when you consider the life of Rufus Porter. He was a sort of "have idea, will travel" man, a jack-of-all-trades who never stayed in one place or at one job for long. Born in West Boxford, Massachusetts, in 1792 and raised in Baldwin, Maine, Porter struck out on his own at the age of twelve. By the time he was twenty, he had already worked as a cobbler, fiddler, house painter, schoolmaster, and private in the Massachusetts Coast Guard. But no job held his interest, and he never stayed long in any one place.

Even the bonds of matrimony could not keep Porter around the house. It wasn't too long after his wedding that Porter took off on a long voyage to the Northwest and Hawaii, leaving his wife and son at home.

For the next twenty years, Porter traveled the countryside, offering to paint palm trees, handsome maples, or elaborate scenes of the hunt on living room walls for a fraction of the price of wallpaper. Porter left his mark on more than one hundred houses in three New England states. In his spare time, he invented things — a revolving almanac, life preserver, fire alarm system, and a washing machine. He sold his plans for a revolving rifle to Samuel Colt.

By 1845, the itinerant painter was ready to try his hand at journalism. That year he bought the *New York Mechanic,* a magazine of science. Soon thereafter, he founded his own paper, the celebrated *Scientific American.*

Four years later, Porter published a famous treatise with a long subtitle: *Aerial Navigation, The practicability of traveling pleasantly and safely from New York to California in three days.* Ahead of his time, Porter had devised a brilliant scheme to airlift passengers to the West in a small-size, high-speed flying machine that would accommodate one hundred persons. Man had not yet learned to fly, and Porter was trying to build the airliner. When he could not raise the capital to build his plane, he built a working model. The model never got off the ground.

Another Father of Flight?

For several decades, the Smithsonian Institution refused to exhibit Wilbur and Orville Wright's plane. The reason? The Smithsonian insisted one Samuel P. Langley of Roxbury, Massachusetts, invented the first airplane capable of manned flight. Of course, the top man at the Smithsonian was at one time . . . well, Samuel P. Langley.

Langley was born in 1834 to a Boston merchant whose hobby was astronomy. As a boy Sam was as familiar with a telescope as other boys are with toy soldiers. It was the foundation for a distinguished career in astronomy. For twenty years, Langley was the director of the Allegheny Observatory in Pennsylvania. He published extensively, and along with colleagues, Langley measured the energy of solar radiation from a station on Mt. McKinley, using an instrument he invented. It came as no surprise to the scientific community when in 1887 he was chosen to be assistant secretary of the Smithsonian. When the incumbent secretary died later that year, Langley became secretary.

Along with his interest in astronomy, Langley was convinced of the feasibility of manned flight. Under the auspices of the Smithsonian, he obtained a grant of fifty thousand dollars from the War Department for the development of a full-size manned aircraft. His friend and colleague Charles D. Walcott assisted him.

The *Aerodrome* was not without merit — its motor was in some respects more advanced than that of the Wrights' — but the plane itself

Samuel P. Langley

Langley's Aerodrome *spent more time in the Potomac than it did in the air.*

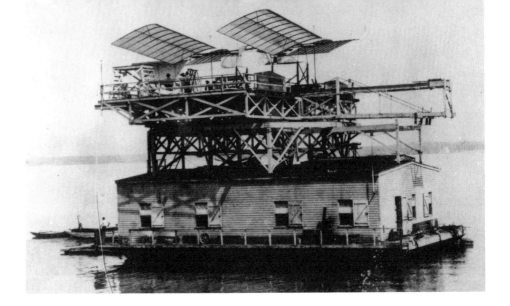

was not airworthy. Nevertheless, in October of 1903, as the Wrights prepared to ship their *Flyer* to Kitty Hawk, Langley mounted his *Aerodrome* atop a houseboat on the Potomac. With the entire eastern press in attendance, the *Aerodrome* fell into the river "like a handful of mortar." The *Boston Herald* suggested that Langley direct his energies to the area of submarines.

Convinced that the difficulty lay with the launching mechanism, the sixty-nine-year-old Langley staked the last of his War Department money on a second launch and tried again in December. On his signal, the *Aerodrome* sped down its sixty-foot track, flipped directly upwards, and plunged once more into the river. Eleven days later, ignored by the press, the Wright brothers accomplished what Samuel Langley had attempted and failed. Langley never properly diagnosed the design faults in his aircraft; he went to his grave only a few years later believing that only a proper launch pad lay between him and destiny.

When Langley died, his position was filled by none other than Charles D. Walcott, Langley's assistant on the *Aerodrome*. Like his mentor, Walcott believed the plane failed only because of the launching mechanism. With Walcott in charge, the Smithsonian refused to acknowledge the Wright brothers' place in history. It was not until 1942 that the Institution offered a belated apology, and in 1948, the *Flyer* was shipped to the museum.

The Domestic Flying Saucer

In the waning years of World War II, a strange pancake-shaped object was sighted in the skies over Connecticut. It looked a little like a flying saucer, but it was not from outer space. The V-173, also known as the Flying Flapjack or the Zimmer Skimmer, was built in Stratford and tested on the runway of Chance-Vought field.

The experimental plane, built by Charles Zimmerman, was designed to take off and land almost vertically, yet fly and fight at high speeds. Had it been successful, every ship in the navy would have carried one, increasing a fleet's striking power and range.

On the November day in 1942 when pilot Boone T. Guyton taxied down the runway, expectations were running high. Zimmerman had devoted thirteen years to the V-173. Electrical models, wind tunnel tests, and the expert opinion of leading aerodynamicists at MIT all said it should fly.

As Guyton knew, it had better. The two engines were underpowered, and due to the long landing gear, it would probably overturn in a forced landing. Constructed entirely of wood, the Zimmer Skimmer could conceivably splinter into toothpicks in a crash. If it touched down in water, the pilot would have a tough time escaping because of the large wing surrounding him. Not only was the design unusual, the newly invented right-angle gear boxes driving the propellers had never been tested in actual flight. As Guyton strapped on the football helmet he wore in case of a crash, everyone wished him luck.

With the throttle full on, the flying saucer lifted off in an incredibly short distance. But just fifty feet into the flight, Guyton knew he was in trouble. The ailerons were not balanced properly, and steering the saucer was akin to directing a truck full of dynamite down a twisting mountain grade just as the brakes give out. Only twelve minutes into the flight he was ninety degrees off course and dead tired from the exertion. Guyton's landing was so short, the Flying Flapjack flipped over.

Charlie Zimmerman could not have been happier. It may not have

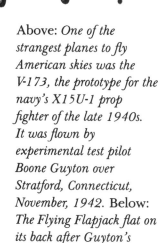

Above: *One of the strangest planes to fly American skies was the V-173, the prototype for the navy's X15U-1 prop fighter of the late 1940s. It was flown by experimental test pilot Boone Guyton over Stratford, Connecticut, November, 1942. Below: The Flying Flapjack flat on its back after Guyton's crash landing in 1942.*

been perfect, but the saucer flew. Over the next five years, the unusual plane was flown by test pilots, curious admirals, even Charles Lindbergh. Work was begun on a more powerful, heavier model.

And then fate intervened: The jet engine was born. As Guyton waited on the runway for the first test flight of the newer model, Zimmerman received a message instructing him to cease all further work on the plane. The V-173 flying wing now resides at the National Air and Space Museum awaiting restoration. The improved model was demolished.

Pfitzner's Flying Wing

Lieutenant Alexander A. Pfitzner was a grave and courteous young man who reminded some of a prim schoolmaster. His specialty was internal-combustion engines, and he came to this country from Budapest early in the century to undertake experimental work for Buick. His talent brought him to the attention of Glenn H. Curtiss, an airplane manufacturer at Hammondsport, New York. The tight-fisted Curtiss was

Lieutenant Alexander A. Pfitzner at the controls of the Burgess-Pfitzner biplane, 1910.

trying to figure out a way to sell airplanes without having to pay a royalty to the Wright brothers, who held the patent on the ailerons that made flight so easy. Over the years, Curtiss had spent an enormous amount of money in litigation trying to prove that his ailerons were different from the Wright design, to no avail. Curtiss told Pfitzner to solve the problem.

Since the Wrights' aileron affected the shape of a wing, the engineer worked out a way to alter its size: At each wing tip he installed a panel designed to slide in or out at a turn of the control wheel. The idea was that the larger wing would exert greater lift, thus banking the plane. (Today, this "variable geometry" is a standard feature on the F-111 and the Boeing supersonic transport.)

With spare parts, Pfitzner built a monoplane. Though he had never before piloted a plane, one day in the winter of 1910 he taxied over the frozen surface of Lake Keuka and took off. The wing performed perfectly, Pfitzner said, after he crashed while attempting a landing.

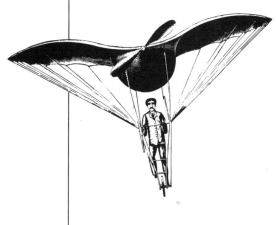

Recovered from his injuries, the lieutenant decided to move on. That spring, he went to work in Marblehead for W. Starling Burgess, Fuller's collaborator on the Dymaxion car. At that time, Burgess and a partner were working on an unusual biplane with six large triangular fins arranged along the top of the upper wing. The design, which proved to be as aerodynamic as a giraffe, was soon dropped in favor of Pfitzner's wing.

In June of 1910, a prototype biplane with a variable wing was transported to Plum Island on Burgess's yacht. Since no professional pilot lived on Plum Island, Pfitzner agreed to fly the experimental craft. His

first attempt began auspiciously enough, but the sliding wings performed erratically. Pfitzner smashed a grain elevator when he attempted to land, and the plane was taken back to the base by cart.

Two more crashes followed before Pfitzner's final flight on July 8. Following an uneventful takeoff, he had flown two miles when one wing dipped without warning. Despite the pilot's frantic efforts, the unstable craft plunged fifty feet into a creek below. Miraculously, the wings struck opposite banks of the creek, and Pfitzner was thrown into the water. Dripping on the bank, he was the picture of dejection. "I wish I'd broken my neck," he said.

Four days later, suitcase in hand, Pfitzner walked down to the Marblehead waterfront and hired a dory. Three hours later, a fisherman found the empty boat drifting two miles from shore. A coat, a hat, and a .32 caliber pistol were in the boat, the latter having been fired very recently. A note stated to whom the boat belonged. The suitcase was gone. Neither Pfitzner nor the drawings of his ill-fated designs were ever seen again.

Cargo Schooners for the Eighties

The first sailing cargo vessel launched in Maine in more than forty years slid down the ways at the R. L. Wallace Shipyard in Thomaston, August 8, 1980, cheered by three thousand spectators and a flag-flying fleet of pleasure boats.

It had taken Edward (Ned) Arthur Ackerman, owner and a self-styled merchant-adventurer, close to a half million dollars and three years to build the *John F. Leavitt,* a ninety-seven-foot, one-hundred-ton wooden vessel named after a curator at Mystic Seaport.

Ned Ackerman

For Ackerman, an intellectual and scholar who at the time was only a dissertation away from his Ph.D. in Old English, Middle English, and Anglo Norman, it was to be the start of a new career — sailing cargo in coastal commerce. And why not? With OPEC ruling the gas pumps and the price of crude oil, the search was on for alternative sources of energy. What could be more practical than the wind, which was both cheap and pollution free? The builder expected to haul lumber, stone, and machinery to island communities along the Maine coast. Like a lot of inspired ideas, this one worked better on paper than on water.

Shortly after the schooner was fitted out, Ackerman sailed her from Maine to Quincy, Massachusetts, to have the elec-

tronic equipment installed and to pick up a cargo of building materials destined for Haiti.

If Ackerman were a superstitious sort, he might have seen as an ill omen the fact that his schooner ran aground within a mile of departing the Wallace Shipyard. Ackerman is not superstitious, and laden with cargo and a documentary film crew on board to record the historic voyage, he departed Quincy on December 19.

The vessel made very slow headway for the first several days for lack of wind. But on December 27, the *John F. Leavitt* was 280 miles southeast of Long Island and in real trouble. Winds had risen to near gale force, seas were running fifteen to eighteen feet, and the ship was taking on water. When one pump was disabled by the storm, the crew sent out a general mayday. At 1:30 P.M., the Coast Guard rescued all nine crew members.

Neither the *Leavitt* nor the cargo was ever found, and Ackerman subsequently retired from boat building. But not all was lost. A film produced about the voyage of the *Leavitt* is now available on video tape.

The first mishap of the John F. Leavitt, *run aground just a mile from the shipyard.*

CHAPTER EIGHT

Improving On Eden

Or How a Yankee Can Refine Nature's Plans

The Maine Coon Cat Is Back

For more than forty years, from 1860 to 1904, the Maine coon cat dominated the feline show world the way the Boston Celtics once pushed around the rest of the National Basketball Association. The first volume of *Cat Fancy of America* registry included twenty-eight Maine coons.

But it is a fickle world, and curiosity about other breeds killed interest in the coon cat. After 1904, the only native American feline dropped out of the public eye, except at home. People in Maine are stubborn about their opinions and not likely to be swayed by the current rage, especially on the superiority of native products. So, while the rest of the nation gushed over the new Persians and Siamese, Mainers maintained their partiality to the native son. In the early 1950s, a few feline fanatics decided coon neglect had gone on long enough and organized the Central Maine (read "Coon") Cat Club. On the sidelines, several groups worked diligently at restoring the coon's reputation in the broader cat world. By 1974, they had succeeded. The C.F.A. once again recognized the coon as a show breed: The cat was back.

The Maine coon does not look like any other cat. For starters, a coon cat is big: There are existing cats weighing in at thirty pounds and fifteen to twenty pounds is quite common. The coat is long and full, and the ears rise in tufted lynx-like splendor from the furry ruff. The legs are sturdy, and the hind legs are frequently embellished with "britches," which look like furry versions of cowboy chaps. The feet look inordinately large, with large tufts between the toes. The tail is a plume carried high like a battle flag. On the subject of color, there are no limits.

Generalities about breeds are dubious at best, and the coon's reputation for being bad-tempered is undeserved. It may be only that twenty pounds of irritable coon cat is more awesome than seven pounds of angry Siamese.

Where exactly the Maine coon cat originated is a matter of some debate, according to Marilis Hornidge, author of *That Yankee Cat: The Maine Coon Cat* (Harpswell Press). One legend involves a chivalrous sea captain whose plan to save a queen failed, but who instead brought to his hometown in Maine a royal breed of feline ("Your kingdom for a cat"). Another revolves around a sea captain named Coon who imported exotic kittens from the Orient. Still another suggests the coon cat is a cross between a raccoon or long-haired lynx and an everyday house cat.

Wherever this breed came from, the Maine coon is at his natural

A Maine coon cat beauty. This is Tamarack's Togo, born of Red Baron and Tamarack's Miss Audacity. Togo was named the best black and white Maine coon cat in the northeast region two years running, 1983 and 1984.

best sitting on a front porch in a small Maine town, his heavy coat gently ruffled by the pine-and-salt-scented wind, washing his big tufted paws after a long day of making sure the world is running on track. If you greet him, he will probably be affable and charming, but not effusive. It is an attitude typical of a native son, a folktale Yankee, or a Maine coon cat.

When Reds Ruled the Roost

The chances of finding a chicken anywhere but in the freezer section of the grocery store in Little Compton, Rhode Island, are about nil. But there was a time when Little Compton ruled the roost of the chicken world, thanks to the Rhode Island Red.

The chicken that spawned the poultry industry was first bred on the farm of Captain William Tripp, a retired sea captain and market man who traded with the sailors at New Bedford harbor. In 1854, New Bedford ships visited ports along the southeastern coast of Asia. On one of these trips, a sailor obtained a red cock. Tripp fancied the rooster and took him home to run with his scrub hens.

Much to his surprise, the chicks produced better meat and more and bigger eggs than Tripp's other hens. For the next thirty years, Tripp bred his hens with the red roosters, known locally as "Bill Tripp's Fowls."

Tripp's crossbreeding experiments were watched with great interest by his neighbors, for by the 1880s Little Compton was home to the largest chicken farm in the nation. Isaac Champlin Wilbour and his son Phillip kept between three thousand and four thousand laying hens on their farm, just across the bay from Cornelius Vanderbilt's Breakers on Newport's Gold Coast. In fact, the whole town depended on the chicken business. The Wilbours, who had developed markets in Providence and Boston, bought every egg they could get their hands on just to meet demand.

On his farm, Isaac Wilbour dreamed of an all-around super chicken, one that not only would produce more eggs and meat, but would do it under the adverse conditions of a New England winter. He bought a few of Bill Tripp's fowls and began his own experiments.

Apparently, he achieved what he was looking for sometime in the early 1890s. Samuel Cushman, a professor from the United States Experimental Station at Kingston, Rhode Island, walked down to the breeding pens and asked Wilbour if he had given any thought to naming a new breed.

"Why wouldn't Rhode Island Reds do?" Wilbour asked.

Apparently, it would do fine. After all, it was a red chicken, from Rhode Island.

Isaac Champlin Wilbour

The distinctive single-combed Rhode Island Red cockerel and pullets.

163

By 1896, Wilbour was advertising Rhode Island Reds in the poultry trade journals, and fifty of the chickens were shipped west to Iowa. In 1901, the American Rhode Island Red Club was formed in Boston.

By then, the name was already an anachronism. Just a few years earlier, Wilbour had died, and his son had sold the farm to enter politics. With the biggest show in town bolting the doors, other farmers soon followed suit. Chicken farms were converted to dairies or sold to wealthy summer people who built palaces where the coops once stood.

In 1925, a bronze plaque commemorating the Red was erected on land donated by Debbie Manchester in nearby Adamsville. The location was something of a controversy since none of the development work on the breed was ever conducted there. As it turned out, the Rhode Island Red Club of America was putting up some of the money, and a group of breeders in Fall River claimed they had developed the all-purpose chicken. Adamsville was about halfway between the two towns. The solution pleased no one. The Rhode Island Red received its highest honor on May 3, 1954, when Governor Dennis J. Roberts designated it as the official state bird.

The Little Horse That Could

Sometime around the turn of the 19th century, a Randolph, Vermont, farmer by the name of Robert Evans came down from his logging fields just as a local log pulling contest was coming to an end. Several big horses, weighing more than 1,200 pounds each, had attempted to move a particular pine log onto a sawmill logway, but none could budge it.

Evans had been working with a small horse named Figure, which he rented from Justin Morgan, a local singing master who often leased out his little stallion. Though Figure stood only fourteen hands tall and weighed less than one thousand pounds, Evans bet one gallon of rum his colt could draw the log onto the logway in just three pulls. As he studied the situation, Evans said he felt ashamed to hitch his animal to such a puny log and suggested that three onlookers have themselves a seat on the log while he and Figure went to work. He was wrong in his estimate. Figure moved the log with just two pulls.

It was not the last contest the little horse that could would win. Figure worked hard for nearly thirty years. But what he did best was reproduce strong, willing, and able colts just like himself. Named for

Figure, the first Morgan horse, has been the subject of numerous prints and etchings.

the teacher who brought Figure to Vermont from Springfield, Massachusetts, in 1789, the Morgan is the oldest of America's light horse breeds.

The Morgan was the utility infielder of the horse world. Figure's offspring wrenched out stumps in Vermont and drew the finest buggies in Manhattan society. In the 1850s, Ethan Allen 50 was the fastest trotter of his day. Morgans distinguished themselves in battle during the Civil War on both sides of the battle lines. "It was your hawses that done licked us!" one confederate soldier is said to have told his captors from the First Vermont Cavalry Regiment. Little Sorel, Stonewall Jackson's Morgan, was "said to eat a ton of hay or live on cobs." A Morgan named Comanche was the only survivor of the infamous Battle of the Little Bighorn.

If it were not for the efforts of Colonel Joseph Battell, a newspaper publisher and innkeeper in Weybridge, Vermont, the Morgan might have died out with the coming of the automobile. Battell hated the car as much as he loved his Morgans — Battell's first and last automobile ride was said to be in the ambulance that carried him to the hospital in 1915 during a fatal illness.

In the late 1800s, Battell devoted a good deal of his time to breeding and promoting the Morgan breed at the Breadloaf Inn, his farm. Along

The horse, Lady de Jarnette, a Morgan, was named the handsomest exhibition horse in America.

with a few other fanatics, he traveled the country to verify pedigrees and bloodlines and in 1894 published the first volume of the *Morgan Horse Register.* In 1906, Battell gave his farm and Morgans to the U. S. Government, which later turned the property over to the University of Vermont. Better than 75 percent of today's Morgans can be traced back to the government horses.

Though the breed now thrives, the story of Figure has a tragic ending. After Justin Morgan died, Figure passed through a series of owners who progressively treated the gallant old stallion with disregard. In 1821, he was kicked in the side by another horse. Exposed without shelter to a northern Vermont winter, the injury killed him. The horse was buried in the pasture of a farm near Tunbridge, Vermont.

The Chinook Dog

Above: *The famous Chinook.* Right: *Laurence Orne, of Melrose, Massachusetts, and his dog, Paugus. These two were named "America's most typical boy and dog" by a dog food company in 1931.*

In 1931, a dog-food company sponsored a publicity contest in search of "America's most typical boy and dog." The winner of half the contest was a Chinook dog from Nashua, New Hampshire, named Paugus.

America's most typical dog breed, the only sled-dog breed created in New England, was a breed developed by Arthur Walden, an adventurer who left New Hampshire for Alaska in the 1890s. There he became a mail-team driver, hauling freight and supplies by dog team in the Klondike. After returning to the quiet New Hampshire village of Wonalancet, he missed the excitement of sledding and scouted the area for the right-sized dogs. In time, he assembled a team of mongrels and used them to give rides to the guests at his wife's resort, Wonalancet Farm.

Around 1917, a litter of three identical yellow puppies was born at the farm. The father was a stray found near the Canadian border of Maine, and the mother a descendant of one of Admiral Peary's sled dogs. The puppies all grew into avid sled pullers, but one of them distinguished himself by his strength and spirit. Walden made him a lead dog and dubbed him "Chinook." When Walden began breeding Chinook to females of predominantly German shepherd background, the results

were large, tawny dogs that looked as if they had all come from the same mold. Chinook was that freak of nature that begets offspring exactly like itself — like the stallion upon which the Morgan horse breed was based.

Walden's breed came to fame in 1922 when the Brown Paper Company of Berlin, New Hampshire, sponsored the first Eastern International Sled Dog Derby. The Chinooks won the three-day race. With his reputation and livelihood assured, Walden created even bigger headlines when he became the first to climb Mt. Washington with a dog team in a blizzard, with winds so ferocious that occasionally one of the heavy Chinooks was lifted off its feet.

As dog-sled racing became more popular in New England, the competition stiffened. By 1927, smaller, speedier Siberian huskies from Alaska and leggier Canadian hound teams were consistently outdistancing the Chinooks, and the breed began to fall out of favor. Once near extinction, they were called the world's rarest breed in 1966 by *The Guinness Book of World Records.* Today, they are making a comeback.

The breed may have fallen out of favor, but the original sire for whom the breed was named lives on in legend and memorial. In 1928, Walden volunteered to accompany Admiral Richard Byrd on his expedi-

Arthur Walden and his lead dog, Chinook. The two were famous enough to draw crowds wherever they went.

169

tion to Antarctica. Though Chinook was semiretired due to advancing age, he was allowed to run freely beside Walden's sled. One day, the dog disappeared. Someone told Walden that Chinook was last seen wandering near the ice fields away from camp. Weeks later, one of the expedition members peered into a deep crevasse. Far below was a ledge marked with paw prints. The sides of the crevasse bore long scratches, as if a big dog had hurled himself from the ledge in an attempt to climb out.

When word of Chinook's disappearance was radioed to the world, it became a front-page story. Later, when New Hampshire officials wanted to rename the road through his town the "Walden Highway," Walden asked that it be called "the Chinook Trail" instead, and so it was. Road signs along Route 113A from Tamworth to Wonalancet still bear the likeness of the gallant dog.

New Dimensions for Day Lilies

At Alna, Maine, the summer stillness was once broken only by the song of meadowlarks and the murmur of hemlocks. Except on the last Saturday of July. On that day, the old Parsons place shook, rattled, and rolled as hundreds of farm folk and summer people exclaimed over and bought some of the most spectacular day lilies in the world, most of them bred right there by the Reverend Dr. Joseph Barth.

For those who know only the common orange day lily that brightens a thousand roadsides, Dr. Barth's hybrids are a pleasant surprise. In his hands, the flower assumed astonishing new dimensions and a startling range of colors: deep red, brilliant orange, dazzling yellow, intense lime, soothing pale lilac, and soft pink.

The creator of this display was a tall, broad-shouldered man with a craggy face. Once the minister at King's Chapel, Boston, in 1971 he gave up the vestments of the pulpit for overalls and work shoes and returned

Joseph Barth displaying some varieties of day lilies he created.

to his roots. "I was born on a Kansas farm and got a feel for the earth between my toes while I was still a boy," he said.

In 1935, Barth took his divinity degree and, knowing he would be called to several churches during his lifetime, determined to find a place to call home. Shortly after his marriage, he and his wife Ramona found an advertisement describing the Parsons place as "a nice place to fix up." A nice place to fall down would have been more accurate.

Once they made it livable, Barth felt the itch to raise flowers that would survive Maine's brutal winters. He found his salvation along the foundation of the house: day lilies. But he thought he could breed better ones, and he was off on what Ramona called his "fine, monomaniacal obsession."

It takes five years for a new hybrid to show its true colors. The cycle began in midsummer when Dr. Barth roamed through his patch and selected the parents he wanted to cross. Before dawn, Barth removed one of the stamens, a slender pale green stalk with a pad of golden pollen at the tip, carried it across the patch to the other prospective parent, and brushed the pollen across the mouth of the second plant's pistil — Alna's own two-hundred-pound bumblebee.

If all the conditions were right, a shiny black seed formed, holding the promise of something new under the sun, a brand-new plant. "I never know what I'll get," Barth said. For fifteen years he tried to produce a blue day lily, even though botanists say it may be impossible.

In mid-September, as the pods began to split, Barth popped the seeds into cans and stashed them in the refrigerator until mid-December, when he planted them in flats. In March, he snipped off the tops of the

Joseph Barth created new hybrids by removing a pollen-bearing stamen from one lily and brushing it across the pistil of a different plant.

new seedlings to a height of about eight inches and put each one into its own peat pot. In late May, he planted them outdoors. From then on, the success of the enterprise was mostly determined by genetics.

Most of Dr. Barth's waking hours were spent in the greenhouse or the garden. And he knew why. "I enjoy seeing my hybrids growing in my neighbors' gardens," he said. "And I dream of growing a new day lily, something bigger or richer in color than any in existence. Or something unusual, a true blue, perhaps."

Glorious Glads

On any Saturday morning in August in the hour just before dawn in Randolph, Vermont, the chances are good that Lee Fairchild, a trim man in his seventies, is up and choosing the best of his gladioli to be entered in a flower show somewhere in the Northeast later in the day. The slim, straight spikes that he chooses hold exquisite flowers, some ruffled, some deep-throated, all of them flared open in a way that is brazenly sensual. He knows that he is the only grower in the world who can show these varieties today because they do not exist anywhere else. Lee Fairchild created every one of them.

Nearly forty years ago, when he was a young Presbyterian minister in Stamford, New York, Lee was looking for the kind of hobby a pastor on the move could carry with him from parish to parish. About that time, a neighbor gave him a dozen gladiolus bulbs of mixed variety. "I can still remember when they first bloomed," he says. "I'd never seen gladiolus before, and I became very excited about them. The next year, I bought two bulbs each of fifty varieties, and when they bloomed I began to see what I could make. From then on it just kept expanding."

The first rush of interest expanded into an avocation that has brought him worldwide recognition as one of the best practitioners of the art of gladiolus hybridization. Today, after experimenting with thousands of gladioli, introducing seventeen new varieties, and writing the definitive book on growing them, Lee is still propagating these showy flowers.

His career has been divided into two parts. In the 1950s and 1960s his new varieties of large glads consistently won national awards and were eagerly bought up by commercial growers for the cut-flower industry. His college education debts and a portion of his children's educations were paid for by gladioli. "The most satisfying part is getting one that goes on for a time," he says. "My Chocolate Chip is thirty-five years old

Lee Fairchild is one of a handful of avocational gladiolus hybridizers. He has produced many new varieties, including the award-winning Jay Vee, a miniature variety.

173

Lee Fairchild pollinating gladioli by brushing the pollen from one plant onto the pistil of another. The result should be a unique cross, perhaps the beginning of a new variety.

and still one of the best."

More recently, after retiring from the pulpit to Vermont, he has concentrated on the development of new strains of miniature flowers for the home gardener. "What I'm doing now is a revival," he says lightly. "Just a retirement venture." But he has achieved the same colorful results with the miniatures as with the large blooms. Jay Vee, one of two varieties he introduced in 1980, became a show winner in the 1981 and 1982 seasons; Bit O' Burgundy, a deep rose-red glad is a popular arrangement flower.

This summer in Vermont, Lee's seedlings will come up again, every one with a number he assigned to it, every one with a lineage he remembers, every one from a cross he thought out. As they flower, he will walk among them, making decisions on which to keep. He will keep very few, and even then he will say he has too many, but his curiosity about the possibilities of those he has chosen will get the best of him. He will plant them again next year, and he will make more crosses, just to see where they will go.

The Art of Iris

Beatrice Warburton has a problem most flower breeders would envy. She has a backlog of hybridized irises ready to be officially introduced like debutantes to iris societies. But her irises must wait in the wings, for Bee has simply run out of names. In christening the seventy-five varieties she has already introduced, she has used up the names of her children and grandchildren. The next generation of Warburtons just are not coming fast enough. So Bee has even resorted to baptizing her latest orange and white creation "George Henry," after the tabby that laps up milk in her Westboro, Massachusetts, home.

Beatrice Warburton

"You may laugh," counters Warburton, a short, spritely lady in her eighties, "but seventy thousand names have already been used for irises, and you can't use them over again. Just try to find one that isn't taken."

Finding the right name for each new iris is an important coda to Warburton's creation, perhaps because her attraction to this species began with a name. "Out on the lawn of my childhood house there was a fabulous plant growing under the roof's downspout. I thought it was the most miraculous thing because it reappeared each spring, year after year. Most magical of all, it bore my name: Princess Beatrice."

In the 1940s, after her children had grown, Bee Warburton was ready to raise a floral family and revive her fascination with the iris. Her interest grew as quickly as her garden. Soon she began to improve upon nature, pushing her beloved iris into hybrids of ever-increasing beauty.

Her aesthetic vision has won awards from the United States, Italy, France — in fact every country that gives them. It has also earned recognition from her peers. Almost every book in the iris section of the library lists Bee Warburton in the index or acknowledgments. Several monographs and one thick volume, *The World of Irises,* bear her by-line.

The ultimate proof of her talent lies in the acre of color and fragrance right outside her window, where irises as American as apple pie stand beside blooms that originated in Russia and Japan. Tall bearded irises nod to their beardless cousins who tower over dwarf varieties peeking through their foliage. Finally, there is a row of Sky and Snow, the product of fifteen years of experimentation. Its strongly contrasting blue petals with white beards is a variety no one else has been able to duplicate.

Despite the uniqueness of many of her hybrids, Warburton does not feel competitive with her fellow breeders. She breeds for her own garden, not for the shows. "Raising irises

combines everything you'd ever want to do," Warburton explains, "working with living things, creating something with your artistic yearning."

The Bean Man of Massachusetts

John E. Withee

It is always pleasant to hold a conversation with someone who really knows his beans, and if it is beans you are interested in, John E. Withee, of Lynnfield, Massachusetts, not only would like to talk to you, he may put you to work.

Withee wants to preserve America's heirloom beans, those older species which are dying out or which never were grown on a very large scale. But you cannot store beans away in a museum and expect them to germinate after more than three or four years. And unlike apple trees, you cannot plant beans and forget about them for thirty or forty years. Beans have to be renewed periodically if a variety is to be saved from extinction, and in his retirement years, Withee has dedicated himself to the task.

On slightly less than an acre of land, he cares for three hundred different varieties of bean. He has even formed a nonprofit organization, Wanigan Associates, Inc., named for the Abnaki Indian word given to the cook shack on a raft which floated on streams during early Maine logging operations. There is a connection: Thoreau wrote that all the beans raised in Massachusetts found a market in Maine logging camps, and beans were an everyday item on the menu in the *wanigan.*

Withee's interest in beans was originally culinary — he has been an avid bean eater since his childhood days in rural Maine. "We were poor," he admits, "and my father dickered with someone for a barrel of yellow-eye beans. We lived on those during the winter. There were six kids in the family, and the bean pot was a big one. We ate beans in every way you could eat beans."

Digging the bean hole on Friday nights fell to Withee, so naturally, when he married and moved to Massachusetts, he went looking for beans. "I wanted some Jacob's cattle beans, but couldn't find any in the market here," he remembers. "It was even hard to find a soldier bean."

The search was on. In northern New Hampshire he was introduced to a bean called marafax. It turned out to be a great baking bean, and Withee wondered how many other little-known varieties might still be located, varieties passed down in a family for generations. True heirloom beans. Gradually the idea took shape that it would be fun to collect and

176

preserve them with a renewal growing plan. And so a hobby was born.

In his efforts to track down heirloom beans, Withee has gotten some interesting contributions. Caseknife beans were known in 1820, and the North Haven red from Connecticut, a small, dusty pink seed, dates to 1700. The black kidney bean is pictured in John Gerard's *The Herball, or generall historie of plants,* published in London in 1597. A woman from Maine even sent him beans supposedly descended from those found in King Tut's tomb. While he doubts the lineage, Withee concedes the bean has a certain fascination.

Since Withee does not have land enough to grow all of the varieties of beans that need renewal, he has about two hundred bean growers working with him; he sends two packets for planting, and at the end of the season, the grower sends the seeds back and gets two more packets for the next year. Along with the beans, Withee mails out the Wanigan's newsletter, which he describes as "strictly beany."

Left: *Delicious Giant climbing beans. Withee finds his growers are less interested in climbing varieties even though they are easy to grow and take less garden space.* Right: *A true heirloom, the North Haven Red was grown in Connecticut as early as 1700.*

Year-Round Harvests

In deep winter Leandre and Gretchen Poisson walk out to their snow-covered garden, lift up the Solar Pods and Solar Cones, odd contraptions that appear to simulate cold frames, and harvest fresh vegetables for their table. Snow has never stopped the inventive Poissons. The sun is stronger than snow, they reason, and if used properly will grow garden-fresh food in winter as well as summer.

At their mountaintop farm in Harrisville, New Hampshire, the

Winter sunlight heats the Poissons' fiber glass "Pods" during the day. The heat is stored in drums of water that gradually release heat at night and keep the vegetables from freezing, even on the coldest nights.

Poissons have adapted traditional French intensive gardening, a method of producing food under glass, to the colder New England climes by making "Pods," small-scale greenhouses, using modern materials, insulating techniques, and imagination. Instead of the heavy breakable glass used by the French, the Poissons fit solar-efficient, double-glazed fiber glass sheets over a four-by-eight-foot framed bed of vegetables. Gardening in snow country has its labors, and since snow doesn't melt on the pods, the Poissons have to keep them shoveled clean, not only to relieve the weight, but also to allow the sun to heat up the soil as well as the drum of water at one end of the pods.

When the temperature drops to minus ten degrees or so, the Poissons actually get a lift from Mother Nature. At this temperature it is simply too cold for clouds and snow. The abundant sunlight heats the mulched soil and the drum of water that stores heat overnight and gradually releases warmth inside the pods.

"Our usual growing season in this part of the country is four months," explains Gretchen. "Now we grow the whole year. So we've tripled our growing season."

"If nobody drives over the pods," adds Leandre, "they'll last fifty years."

During most years, February 15 is the first date for planting from seed. At this time, they sow lettuce, radishes, carrots, and onions. By March 15, all cool-loving vegetables germinate and grow well. By April 15, the soil is sufficiently warm to seed heat-loving plants such as tomatoes, peppers, eggplants, melons, and cucumbers.

Although many cool-hardy plants will not grow through the entire winter, the Poissons are still harvesting spinach, Swiss chard, celery, beets, and cauliflower until December 15. By then, it is almost time to start over.

The couple is publishing a book called *American Intensive Gardening,*

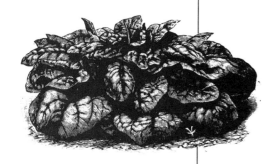

and they plan to visit with gardeners in Europe. "I'm really looking forward to introducing this in France," Leandre says.

No Stony Soil for This Yankee Farmer

Among his many talents, Thomas Gaucher is an oceanographer with an international reputation in submarine and spacecraft life-support systems, a man whose expertise has been called upon to troubleshoot gold mining offshore the Fiji Islands and to reintroduce scallops to Connecticut's Niantic River. What is a man like this doing growing tomatoes in the little town of Lebanon, Connecticut?

He is trying to increase the world's production of food. On his hydroponic farm, Gaucher has adapted aquaculture to the harsh New England climate, growing vegetables year-round in climate-controlled greenhouses without soil, by using a nutrient water solution.

It is an experimental farm, but according to Gaucher, high-density hydroponic farming may hold the key to dramatically increasing food production on land. At present, conventional farming methods result at most in about thirty thousand pounds of food annually per acre — an amount achieved only in warm climates such as southern California. Even in its infancy, aquaculture makes it possible to produce from one to

The Gauchers pick only ripe tomatoes. Their tomatoes cost more at the market, but they sell faster than imported tomatoes because they taste homegrown.

two million pounds per acre.

Gaucher began his experiment in aquafarming in 1972 when he bought an old dairy farm in Lebanon. The idea was his wife's. The stock market decline of the early 1970s knocked out the fringe activities of many corporations that might have hired Gaucher as an oceanographic consultant. It seemed to Mrs. Gaucher to be a good time to settle down somewhere and go into another business. In February of 1973, the pair floated their first crop of 1,100 hybrid tomato plants. The first harvest of five hundred tomatoes was ripe by May 10. In the stores, they discovered a ready market with consumers willing to pay extra for tomatoes fresh off the vine.

It sounds easier than it actually was. The tomatoes were planted in washed and sterilized coarse gravel placed in trays through which the nutrient solutions were pumped. Electronic sensors in the gravel determined the moisture content and turned the pumps on and off as needed. The nutrient solutions contained sixteen essential growth elements, varied according to the crop.

After experimenting with tomatoes, Gaucher expanded the farm into a larger half-acre greenhouse and began to grow hydroponic lettuce and cucumbers. In the future, he anticipates a crop of shrimp, perhaps grown in pools interconnected with the hydroponic system. He has also entertained the possibility of raising fish in the warm water overflow from the coolant systems of nuclear power plants and has grown scallops in the discharge waters of the Millstone power plant.

Whether or not the ventures can be profitable is the next question for Gaucher. "I don't know if they can," he says. "I hope mine will."

Dr. Galinat at work in a greenhouse at the Waltham Field Station.

The Man Who Knows Everything About Corn

A stand of corn is about as natural as Frankenstein's monster and a lot more dangerous, at least potentially," says Dr. Walton C. Galinat, a research professor at the University of Massachusetts.

No, the Pentagon is not developing some new weapon from corn-on-the-cob. The potential danger is economic. "Corn is the basis upon which every North and South American civilization has been built," Galinat explains. "The loss of one year's crop would create economic chaos. And that would be only the beginning." Considered the world's foremost authority on corn, Galinat should know.

The problem is genetic. Over the years, corn has been crossbred to produce better crop yields. In the process much of the natural resistance to pests and disease has been lost. "Guess what would happen if a common corn pest suddenly developed a resistance to our standard insecticides?" Galinat asks. "Wham! Just like that the backbone of American agriculture is broken."

In his laboratory, Galinat is attempting to reproduce ten thousand years of corn evolution. By crossing corn's most primitive relatives, he hopes to duplicate extinct varieties that may hold the answer to disease and pest control. If he is right, and if he can successfully develop high-yield varieties resistant to disease and insects, he could do away with pesticides and revolutionize corn agriculture.

While working on tomorrow's revolution, Galinat has solved mundane problems not quite as dire as the survival of the human species. For instance, one type of Galinat corn grows the world's largest ear — almost two feet long, ideal for many developing countries where most farm work is performed manually, and rows of corn are alternated with beans or squash in the same field. Because the intercropped corn plants are widely spaced, they have a potential to develop large ears.

For denture wearers and corn aficionados tired of flossing after barbecues, Galinat developed Golden Happiness, the first glume-less variety of corn. The glume is the part that always sticks in your teeth.

Freezing corn-on-the-cob has its drawbacks. Not only does it take up a lot of room in the freezer, but the inner part of the thick cob adds a distasteful cardboard-like flavor to the whole ear. Galinat's answer: Candy Stick, a new variety with a cob thinner than a pencil.

How about "airplane corn," a small, light ear with just two rows of kernels on each side? "It's so flat it won't roll off an airline tray," Galinat says with a chuckle. His crowning achievement may be a new variety of sweet corn. Whereas most corn-on-the-cob loses its flavor within a day after picking, the new Galinat strain ages like wine. "It actually grows sweeter with age," Galinat says.

181

CHAPTER NINE

Crime & Punishment

Some Made Better Traps;
Some Made Better Escapes

Confessions of a Black Sheep

In 1807, an aspiring printer from Dover, New Hampshire, published a memoir entitled *A Narrative of the Life, Adventures, Travels and Sufferings of Henry Tufts*. It was a charmingly bizarre document — charming because of its rococo style, full of French quotations and classical allusions; bizarre because of its subject, for Henry Tufts was not a gentleman or a scholar, but the greatest horse thief and all-around knave that colonial New England ever produced.

When George Washington complained of the sunshine soldiers who "consumer your provisions, exhaust your stores, and leave you at last at a critical moment," he was talking about Henry, who spent his Revolution enlisting, deserting, and then dodging the bounty hunters who pursued deserters. When Samuel Beck wrote about the poor malefactors who were bound to the red whipping post that sat in the middle of State Street, Boston's busiest thoroughfare, he might have been describing Henry, who was whipped frequently in his apprentice years as a thief. When the scholars of colonial America note that approximately one-third of all children born were illegitimate, they are saluting the romantic exertions of Henry, a backwoods Casanova. In his eighty-three years he managed to juggle three official wives, several unofficial ones, and a number of extracurricular engagements that ended shy of the altar. He fathered thirteen acknowledged children and untold others, usually mentioned in an aside as his reason for quitting such and such a town.

Timothy Dwight, a contemporary who went on to become president of Yale, had Henry in mind when he wrote: "These men cannot live in regular society. They are too idle; too talkative; too passionate; too prodigal; and too shiftless to acquire either property or character. Finding all their efforts vain, they become at length discouraged: and then under the pressure of poverty, the fear of a gaol, and consciousness of public contempt, leave their native places, and betake themselves to the wilderness."

Henry Tufts became a member of this vagabond class by inclination, not birth. By birth he was a Boston blueblood, albeit somewhat diluted, and he himself described his childhood as a happy, well-behaved one. His "genius," as he called it, began to bloom when he was only fourteen, manifesting itself in raids on neighboring orchards and chicken coops, exploits that most were willing to overlook as youthful high spirits. But then he stole some money from a neighbor, was caught, and publicly disgraced.

Henry Sr., despairing of his son, disinherited him. Whereupon

Henry Jr. stole his father's horse and sold it for thirty dollars.

It is significant, given his ancestry, that Tufts chose horses as his specialty: Like treason, horse stealing was a gentleman's crime, which may
simply be another way of saying that the reward/risk ratio appealed to
those who aspired toward the finer things in life. And Henry enjoyed
life's pleasures. More than once he squandered his loot on brocade
waistcoats, gold watches, and flashing rings. But sartorial extravagance
was impractical when one had to flee along muddy cart tracks or sleep in
haymows or, as he did once, in a family tomb. Henry usually acquired
his clothes from the clotheslines that crossed his path. If his shoes gave
out, he watched for a cobblery. When his purse ran low, he stole a horse.

Henry was no stranger to the jails of New England. "Horris man-
sions" was his name for them, though most were ramshackle structures
in need of constant upkeep. His introduction to them came when he was
still in his teens, when a pregnant girlfriend had him arrested after he
broke his promise to marry her. But that was a mere peccadillo — ten
dollars got the charges dropped. His first serious imprisonment occurred
a year or so later in the territory of Maine. There Henry had met his first
criminal tutor, a man named Dennis, and together they had broken into
and stripped a village store clean. This was a serious offense, as burglars

sometimes received the death penalty. Captured within twenty-four hours, they were lodged in the Portland jail.

It was freezing. It took considerable begging, but finally the jailer consented to let them have a fire. Henry subsequently burned the jail to the ground.

A few months later, after another unsuccessful robbery, Henry ended up in the jail in Essex, New Hampshire, chained to a staple in the floor. This time his punishment was twenty-five lashes and a fine, in lieu of which he and his new accomplice, Smith, would be sold as indentured servants. But when Henry was put up for sale, no one would bid. He escaped from that jail, as well as countless others.

It is evident from his memoirs that Tufts derived enormous pleasure from his deceptions. He thought himself brighter than his fellow colonials, and he probably was. He was a thief not from necessity (at least initially), but because a rambling, dissolute life style appealed to him. In his own way he pursued excellence at his nefarious trade with a passion worthy of Ben Franklin.

The Burglar Alarm

In 1858, E. T. Holmes, a Boston detective (presumably no relation to Sherlock), invented the first practical electronic burglar alarm. Windows and doors were rigged to an electrical contact and wired to a central system. If a thief forced open an entrance, a spring was tripped that completed the electrical contact, and an indicator in the central office would show which house or business was being robbed. In Boston, Holmes's service was popular with the well-to-do and with banks. It also proved to be one of the first practical applications for the telephone, doubling as a telephone switchboard.

While Bell's new invention heralded the coming of a new age of communication, Bell and company faced daunting challenges in developing a market for the phone. Who would use it, and to what end? In 1876, while Bell was on his honeymoon, Gardiner Hubbard, Bell's early benefactor and recent father-in-law, took over the promotion of the telephone. At the time, Charles Williams, the Boston-based electrical whiz in whose shop Bell had developed the invention, discussed the telephone with Holmes, who suggested linking telephones to his wires.

Hubbard at once lent Holmes twelve telephones. He nailed them up in six banks that used his alarm system. One banker made him take

The first telephone switchboard was put to use in Boston in 1877, as part of a burglar alarm system.

185

his "playtoy" out, but the others remained and were used by the bankers to communicate with one another during the day, when it was assumed that nefarious sorts would be in hiding. The wires all ran to a crude switchboard that Holmes rigged up in his office. In effect this was the world's first telephone switchboard, though it was not a public affair like the one in New Haven, Connecticut, years later. At night, the switchboard was returned to its original duty, as a monitor for Holmes's burglar alarms.

A Device We Could Do Without

In the summer of 1905, William McAdoo, police commissioner of New York City, was driving his car through the New England countryside at his usual pace of twelve miles an hour. In the course of that afternoon ramble, McAdoo discovered that the genius of New England had produced still another scientific marvel — the automobile speed trap. It was one Yankee invention we might all live without.

At the turn of the century rural New Englanders took a jaundiced view of the motorcar, generally regarding the gas buggy as just another creation of the devil. In 1902, Vermont passed a law requiring that a grown man waving a red flag must walk ahead of every automobile while it was in motion.

Liberal Massachusetts had a more tolerant view of the horseless carriage, but not by much. As McAdoo approached one small Bay State village, he found the road blocked by what looked like an old-fashioned tollgate. A determined-looking constable named Peabody informed McAdoo he was under arrest. The crime: traveling twelve miles an hour in an eight-mile-an-hour zone.

Before driving McAdoo over to the local magistrate's quarters, Peabody explained his masterpiece. Its principal components were a couple of lookout posts, camouflaged as dead tree trunks, spaced one mile apart. A deputy equipped with a stopwatch and a telephone kept watch for speeders through a knothole. When one went by at a suspiciously rapid rate, the deputy pressed his stopwatch and telephoned ahead to his confederate, who immediately synchronized his watch. When the offender passed, the cop consulted a speed-mileage chart. If the automobile was exceeding the speed limit, he telephoned ahead to another constable manning the road block. Gotcha!

McAdoo was positively exhilarated by his arrest. Immediately, he proposed that the Bay State lawman bring his cronies to New York and install their equipment in the center of automotive traffic law violations. In short order, Peabody and company were apprehending speeders on Upper Broadway in the vicinity of 197th Street. On their first day, they nabbed more speeders than they had bagged in two months back home. After three weeks, the situation was so well in hand that Peabody returned to Massachusetts to resume his protection of the local fauna and general peace of mind of Yankee farmers.

The Perfect No-Nonsense Gadget

The local police in Dover, New Hampshire — as they do all over the country — rely on radar to catch unwary speeders whizzing through town.

The radar gun, an all-seeing eye that never blinks, is the bane of anyone who has ever tried to get from here to there in a hurry. Over the years, ingenious methods have been devised to beat it: aluminum foil in hubcaps, draped from axles, or wadded up between the radiator and the grille, to name a few. But traffic radar is rarely fooled. The perfect no-nonsense gadget, it comes as little surprise to find that it was invented by a Yankee.

In 1947, John Barker, a young engineer at Automatic Signal Corporation, in Norwalk, Connecticut, was trying to use radar to regulate traffic lights automatically. The project was stuck because of the Doppler effect — when reflected from a moving object, like an automobile, the frequency of the radar radio signal changed, and the radar just wouldn't work.

The change in the signal, however, could be measured. In the device Barker perfected, a radar antenna is mounted near the edge of the pavement, where it transmits a sharp, horizontal beam of radio waves down the highway. In this position, the radio signals begin to bounce from any car that enters the beam at a point approximately five hundred feet from the antenna. The reflected signals are fed into a "speed meter," an electronic speedometer that translates them into actual speed with an accuracy of plus or minus two miles per hour. Interestingly enough, radar will never clock you faster than you are going; it will always read slightly less than your real speed.

Radar evidence is accepted in the courts today almost without question, thanks to the Connecticut Supreme Court. In 1966, a driver objected that during his trial no expert testimony had been given as to the accuracy of radar. Supreme Court Justice James E. Murphy disagreed. "From now on," ruled the judge, "anyone who is caught speeding by radar is automatically guilty."

Clarence A. Adams

Escape by Hypnosis

For more than fifteen years, the town of Chester, Vermont, was plagued by a rash of petty thefts. Occasionally a drifter was sent off to prison, but the crimes continued unabated. By 1902, the owner of the gristmill had had enough. On July 29, he rigged a gun full of shot near an entrance favored by the thief. The next morning, the gun had been fired, and blood indicated the charge had found its mark.

Clarence A. Adams was the last person anyone would have suspected. Chief trustee of the library, he had at one time served as a selectman and member of the legislature. Yes, Adams privately collected volumes on hypnotism, the occult, magic, and necromancy. But this was just the eccentric hobby of a gentleman farmer. Still, Adams was discovered in bed with a charge of shot in his left leg. He confessed to all the burglaries. Robbery, he said, "was great sport." Adams was sentenced to ten years in the State Prison at Windsor.

In prison, where he worked in the library, Adams seemed to be the model prisoner. But the day he set foot in jail, Adams began to plan an escape as weird as the mystical books he read so voraciously. Together with the convict physician, who was also a lover of books, he devised a plan whereby he would die a prisoner and be reborn a free man. The only obstacle was the visiting physician from the outside, who was required to sign the death certificates of all men who perished inside the prison walls.

On Washington's Birthday in 1904, Adams told the visiting physician he could feel the grippe coming on and was certain he would die soon. Dr. Brewster ordered him to bed and placed him in the care of the convict physician. Three days later, the prison doctor announced that Adams had died of pneumonia. He made out a death certificate and sent it with his report of treatment to Dr. Brewster, who signed it immediately. In the meantime, the prison doctor laid out the body himself, washed the corpse, removed it to a slab in the side room, and covered it with sheets and a blanket.

Though Adams had scores of relatives in Chester, he left behind a hastily drawn will in which he left his body to a certain William Dunn. Dunn appeared at the prison to take charge of the body almost before it was cold. After a brief ceremony, Adams was laid in a casket and driven to Cavendish, where he was stored in a vault for burial in the spring after the ground had thawed.

Two months later, a well-known traveling man returned from a trip to Canada where he said he had talked to Adams in Nova Scotia. The

casket was opened, and a body was found inside. Due to decomposition it was impossible to tell exactly whose body it was, and the sexton quickly buried the coffin in Adams's cemetery plot.

When Adams was again seen in Canada a few months later, the people of Chester demanded an investigation, and the newspapers sent up a hue and cry. Suddenly, the story was dropped, and Adams's relatives refused permission to have the body exhumed. No investigation was ever made.

So what really happened? According to a prison story told years later, Adams had learned how to put himself into a hypnotic state of suspension that resembled death. While in that state, his friend went so far as to stuff his ears and nasal passages with cotton, as was the custom, but in such a way as to allow a passage of air. Adams gambled that by faking death in February, his body would not be buried until spring. Old friends removed the vault locks with a screwdriver and revived Adams. A cadaver purchased from the medical school at Dartmouth College was substituted for the prisoner. Adams then traveled overland to a remote railway station and escaped to Canada. Later still, he drifted to Mexico, where all trace of him was lost.

Lizzie Borden

Lizzie Borden Took an Ax . . .

Lizzie Borden took an ax
and gave her mother forty whacks
And when she saw what she had done,
She gave her father forty-one.

Actually, Mrs. Borden received only nineteen whacks, but who is counting? Nearly a century after the brutal attack, no one really knows who swung the ax on the sweltering morning of August 4, 1892.

Shortly after nine o'clock that day, tight-fisted Andrew Borden left

Top: *A rare scene-of-the-crime photograph. Andrew Borden lays slain on a couch in the Borden home.*
Bottom: *This ax, presumably the murder weapon, was found concealed in the wall by two workmen in 1949, when the old Borden homestead was being renovated.*

his house at 92 Second Street for a walk. The Bordens were a moderately wealthy and rather stodgy family in Fall River, Massachusetts. Borden had two spinster daughters by his first wife, then dead nearly thirty years. Emma, forty-one, was visiting that day in nearby Fairhaven. Lizzie, thirty-two and active in the church, was at home along with Abby Borden, her stepmother, and Bridget Sullivan, the maid.

When Borden returned from his walk sometime before eleven o'clock, Bridget fumbled with the bolt and double locks before she could open the front door (the home was a fortress). Watching from the stairs, Lizzie laughed and joined them in the downstairs sitting room. She remarked that Mrs. Borden had received a note from a friend and had gone out. When Bridget asked who was sick, Lizzie replied that she did not know, but "it must be someone in town."

Very soon after, Andrew Borden lay down for a nap on the couch. Bridget went to her attic room for a short rest, and Lizzie, by her testimony, walked to the barn at the rear of the yard in search of fishing line.

As Lizzie told it, she was gone only a few minutes. Upon her return, she found the wall, the floor, and her father spattered with blood. While the maid hurried across the street for a physician, Lizzie remained behind, even though an ax murderer may have been lurking in the next room.

Within minutes, several persons reached the house. Lizzie told them she thought she had heard her stepmother come in. Upstairs, Mrs. Borden was found in the guest room, sprawled on her face on the bloodstained floor. Later, medical evidence proved that she preceded her husband in death by at least an hour. While Mr. Borden had been attacked from the rear, Mrs. Borden was struck as she faced her assailant.

Neither bloodstained clothing nor the murder weapon was ever found. And even with the offer of a five-hundred-dollar-reward, no one claimed to have delivered a note to Mrs. Borden. Lizzie was the prime suspect. Several possible motives were put forth: She allegedly hated her stepmother; she was frustrated by her father's parsimony; along with her sister, she stood to inherit an estate worth three hundred thousand dollars.

Ten months after the murder, a period she spent in jail, Lizzie stood trial. Following thirteen days of testimony, the jury returned a verdict of "Not Guilty" on little more than an hour's deliberation. No one has proved otherwise. With their inheritance, the Borden sisters lived quietly in Fall River until their almost simultaneous deaths in 1927.

The Brink's Holdup

At the time, it was the biggest stickup ever. In less than twenty minutes, seven gunmen scooped up 1,200 pounds of cash plus checks and money orders worth more than $2.5 million from the Boston headquarters of Brink's, Inc. For years it looked like the perfect crime. Then suddenly, with the statute of limitations about to run out, Joseph "Specs" O'Keefe squealed on his partners in crime. With only four days to spare, a Suffolk County grand jury handed down indictments.

The mastermind behind the Brink's job was "Fat Tony" Pino, an alien from Sicily who operated a diner. Pino's previous crimes ranged from child molestation to stealing a dozen golf balls. For eighteen months, the gang of eleven studied every possible detail of the Brink's operation: They memorized the alarm system and duplicated keys to the doors that led to where the money was stored. They even held several dry runs through the Brink's operation, padding about in their stocking feet right under the guards' noses.

THEY SHOULD HAVE CALLED HIM GRUMPY

In 1937, Alfred Brady, Public Enemy Number One, was blasted into eternity on Central Street in Bangor, Maine. Brady had led his notorious gang of small caliber bank robbers (at five feet five inches, Brady was the tallest — his prison nickname was Dopey) to Maine to evade an FBI dragnet and buy weapons in "the only state where they don't want your whole life story when you go in to buy a gun," as one of the survivors put it. Unfortunately, the gang's request for a machine gun aroused suspicions even there. In a thirty-second gun battle during which at least sixty shots were fired, FBI agents killed Brady and one of his henchmen. Brady's body now lies in an unmarked grave in Bangor.

On the evening of January 17, 1950, they were ready. Nine men piled into the rear of a green stake-body truck stolen nearly a year earlier just for this occasion. Seven of the men donned Navy pea coats, chauffeur's caps, and Halloween masks. Gloves masked fingerprints while crepe-sole shoes and rubbers muffled the sounds of their feet. All were roughly the same height and weight — distinguishing one bad guy from the other would be impossible.

By the time the truck arrived at the Brink's Prince Street headquarters, two watchmen were already in place. When the all-clear signal was given by flashlight, the seven used their keys to make their way through five doors leading to the second-floor vault. Busy counting the day's receipts, the guards surrendered without a fight. In just less than

twenty minutes, the burglars were on their way with the loot. Two months later, the truck, which had been cut into tiny pieces with a torch, was found buried in the town dump at Stoughton, Massachusetts, near Specs's house.

The details of the Brink's job were more or less known for years. Joseph Drineen, a *Boston Globe* reporter who got to know the crooks, even wrote a book about the robbery thinly disguised as fiction. Still, there was absolutely no legal evidence to tie anyone to the heist.

Not, that is, until Specs O'Keefe started to sing. According to Specs, he was cheated out of sixty-two thousand dollars when the loot was divvied up. After he complained, he was shot at twice in the streets. Later, a bookie close to Specs disappeared; Specs took the hint. When in 1955 he found himself incarcerated for a parole violation, he got to thinking about all those bullets and decided to talk. As a result of O'Keefe's confession, ten of the original eleven went to jail for life. Two died in prison. On a June morning in 1960, Specs walked out of a Pennsylvania courthouse a free man. The money has never been found.

Above: *"Fat Tony" Pino* (center). Previous page: *Joseph "Specs" O'Keefe.*

CHAPTER TEN

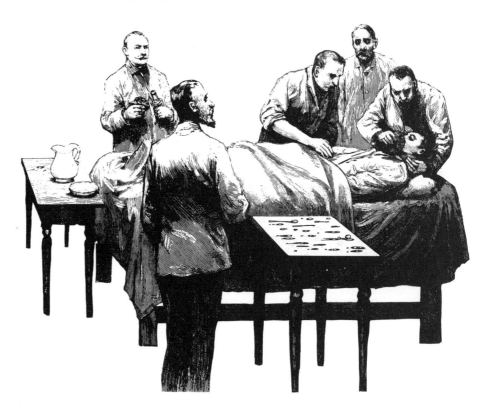

Life & Death Decisions

From Gatling Guns to Iron Lungs

Undersea Adventures

In 1771, David Bushnell, a twenty-seven-year-old Yale freshman from Saybrook, Connecticut, went down to the river with a container full of explosives. One of his instructors had stated that gunpowder would not explode underwater, and Bushnell decided to see for himself. The gunpowder not only exploded, but the force of the blast was increased by the density of the water.

Bushnell decided there was a great future in underwater explosive devices that could be attached to the keels of warships. To attach them without being spotted, he invented the submarine.

He called his craft *The American Turtle.* Built in 1775 in his hometown of Saybrook and tested on the Connecticut River, the first submarine looked to the inventor like Siamese turtle shells attached at the belly. An odd, egg-shaped contraption measuring six feet high, it could hold one man and enough air for thirty minutes under water.

The *Turtle* had two hand-operated propellers that drove it forward and backward or up and down. A rudder maneuvered the craft, and two foot-powered pumps admitted water into the ballast for submersion or pumped it out to rise. The control panel included a pressure-operated depth gauge and a compass. A large screw was used to set the underwater mine in place — when the sub backed away, a timing device was tripped.

With the backing of George Washington, the *Turtle* went into battle in 1776 in New York Harbor. The British fleet had gained control of the Hudson River in order to cut New England off from the other colonies. With a soldier named Ezra Lee at the controls, the *Turtle* slipped into the water under the cover of night to take on the H.M.S. *Eagle,* a fifty-gun frigate.

Lee submerged underneath the *Eagle,* but the submarine's wooden

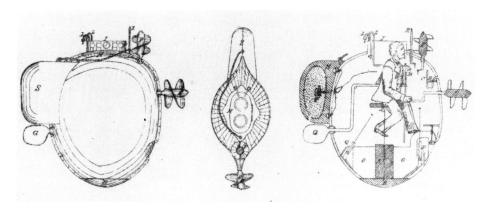

Bushnell's American Turtle, *the submarine used in a failed attempt to destroy the British fleet in the New York Harbor in 1776.*

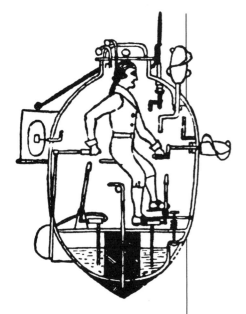

An artist's rendering showing how the soldier fit inside and operated The American Turtle.

Samuel Colt

screw would not bite into the ship's copper bottom. With his air supply gone, Lee finally had to surface, but by that time, dawn was breaking, and a patrol boat noticed him bobbing at the surface. Frantically, Lee submerged again and released the mine to create a diversion. It exploded, no damage was reported, and Lee escaped to safety.

A few weeks later, Lee attempted to blow up another ship. This time he was swept away by the tide while he was submerged. A few months later, the *Turtle* was sunk by cannon fire. Though Bushnell later retrieved it, his sub never saw action again and may have been destroyed to keep it out of British hands. The only drawings that survived of the submarine were produced by the navy in 1885 — Bushnell never wrote a description of his craft.

The Gun That Won the West

It would come as no surprise to anyone who knew him as a boy that Samuel Colt invented "the gun that won the West." To say the least, his was an explosive childhood.

Colt was born near Hartford, Connecticut, in 1814. Soon after, his father moved the family to Ware, Massachusetts, where he opened a silk mill. At the precocious age of ten, Colt began to experiment with the submarine mines invented by Robert Fulton and set one off in a local pond, drenching the onlookers with muddy water. His formal schooling ended after a failed year at Amherst Academy, where he set off an explosion that burned school property. Not knowing what else to do with the boy, Colt's father shipped him off to sea on the brig *Corlo*. Colt was only twelve at the time. Gun making would never be the same as a result of that voyage.

The ship sailed to Calcutta, India, where Colt saw one of the repeating pistols invented by Elisha Collier, a Bostonian who had moved to London when American manufacturers showed little interest in his weapon.

During the return voyage to Boston, Colt worked out the details for his own repeating six-shooter. A pawl mechanism rotated and locked the cylinder in place by the action of cocking the hammer, while a revolving cylinder held the charges. The mechanics were so simple that Colt was able to whittle his first model from wood, using a hot wire to burn the cylinder holes. He was still in his early teens.

Everyone admired the ingenuity of Colt's six-gun. But the consen-

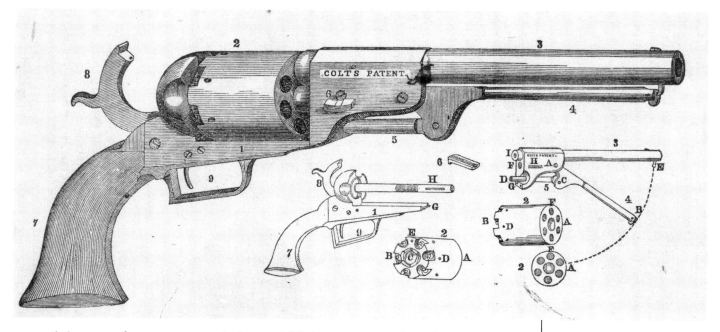

Colt's Patent Repeating Pistol, the gun that won the West.

sus opinion was that no one needed a rapid firing weapon when the country was at peace. To raise the capital to patent his gun, Colt traveled the country giving "scientific lectures" under the pseudonym of Dr. Coult. The highlight of an evening of scientific babble was a demonstration of the effects of laughing gas on the audience.

In 1836, Colt received an American patent for his pistol and opened the Patent Arms Manufacturing Company in Paterson, New Jersey. A few of his guns sold — the army bought fifty to use in the fight against the Seminole Indians in Florida, and the Texas Rangers bought a few — but the company officers were not willing to finance the machine tools needed to produce the weapons cheaply. By 1843, the company was bankrupt.

For the next few years, Colt earned a living in a variety of ways. He perfected a submerged mine exploded by an electrical impulse and laid an underwater telegraph line from New York to Coney Island and Fire Island.

His fortunes unexpectedly changed in 1846 with the start of the Mexican War. Early in the fighting, a few Americans were ambushed by Mexicans. Captain Thornton, the only survivor, fought his way out of the ambush with his Colt revolvers. When news of the gun battle reached General Zachary Taylor, he ordered one thousand revolvers. Though he had no plant, Colt accepted the order and asked Eli Whitney, Jr., to manufacture them for him at the Whitneyville factory. A year later, Colt hired Elisha King Root, known then as the best mechanic in New England, and opened the Colt Patent Arms plant at Hartford. Together, they created the first true assembly line.

A worker drilling holes in a receiver at the Colt plant in Hartford, Connecticut.

Business success did not translate into Colt's personal life. One of his sisters committed suicide by swallowing arsenic, and a brother was imprisoned after one of the mid-century's most celebrated murders. Colt did not marry until he was in his forties. In 1862, while in the midst of intense production for the Civil War, he died suddenly. He was only forty-eight years old.

A Weapon to End All Wars

First and foremost, Dr. Richard Jordan Gatling was a man of peace. Early on in the Civil War, he saw the first of the wounded soldiers coming home, some never to walk, others never to work or see the stars again. The horror of it all touched him deeply. In his effort to end all wars, he invented a weapon so terrible he was certain that men would hesitate to use it against their fellow men. It did not work out that way.

Gatling was born in 1818 in North Carolina, the son of an inventor. Early on he helped his father make a machine for sowing cotton seed, followed by a machine for thinning plants. As a young man finding his way in the world, Gatling taught school, ran a store, and invented a screw propeller before he found his calling as an inventor of farming equipment. His first important invention was a rice-sowing machine patented in 1844, later adapted for sowing wheat.

He was a prosperous manufacturer in the winter of 1845 when he came down with smallpox while on board a river boat. Caught on the ice on the Ohio River for two weeks, Gatling was unable to get medical care. When he recovered from his illness, he studied medicine in Cincinnati so that he and his family would never be without treatment in an emergency. Though he became a physician, he never practiced medicine.

By the time the Civil War started, Gatling had factories in a number of cities turning out his machinery. As he tried to imagine a weapon horrible enough to end all wars, he came up with the first practical machine gun: ten barrels cranked by hand, rotated around a central axis. An ammunition hopper mounted over the breech supplied new bullets as each barrel passed underneath. The Gatling gun would fire as long as the gunner could crank the handle, as many as 1,200 shots a minute.

Top: *Dr. Richard Jordan Gatling and his famous gun.* Left: *The Gatling gun had its first use during the Civil War by Union soldiers.*

His first batch of weapons was destroyed in a fire, and a second lot did not interest the military. But in 1865, just before the end of the war, the Gatling gun was adopted by the U. S. Government and put into service.

But it did not end wars. Instead, other inventors improved on the Gatling gun, turning out even more horrible weapons. Following the Civil War, Gatling lived in Hartford, Connecticut, where he sold his patent rights to the Colt Company. Like the man who beat his sword into a plowshare, Gatling returned to his first love and invented a motorized plow. He died in New York in 1903.

The Great Equalizer of World War II

The bazooka is so simple and yet so powerful," Major General L. H. Campbell, Jr., once said, "that a foot soldier using it can stand his ground with the certain knowledge that he is the master of any tank which may attack him."

Whether or not the general ever personally stared down an oncoming tank armed only with his trusty bazooka is a matter of speculation. The anecdotal evidence is on his side: Like Candy Cummings's curveball and little David's slingshot, the bazooka was the Great Equalizer of World War II.

The idea for armor-piercing weaponry had been around since the

A soldier demonstrating the proper way to hold the bazooka.

1890s. It was not until the Germans deployed a virtually unstoppable tank corps in Africa that the urgency to develop it arose. American infantry had nothing with which to combat them effectively. The foot soldier's rocket launcher took priority over all other ordnance projects.

On a May morning in 1942, a couple of General Electric engineers arrived at the Bridgeport Works with preliminary sketches and models of a proposed new weapon, the "Launcher, Rocket, AT, M-1." The army wished GE to "design, develop, and produce" five thousand of them within thirty days. Under ordinary circumstances, development alone would have required six months. Five days later, the first prototype was delivered to the army for testing.

The rocket launcher was essentially a tube approximately 2½ inches in diameter and five feet long, with open ends, equipped with sights and an electric firing device. A rocket was inserted through one end, the tube was placed in firing position over the right shoulder of the soldier, and it was aimed at the target. Simple! At eighteen pounds, the new weapon was so light it could easily be handled by two men, one in a pinch, yet it fired a projectile that could knock out a tank. Soldiers dubbed it the "bazooka" after a strange musical instrument made famous by comedian Bob Burns.

On Day 22, the army approved the bazooka for production. Just over a week remained in which to manufacture five thousand of them. Steel was transported around the clock from Pittsburgh to Bridgeport by truck and by air. The bazookas were loaded into trucks and shipped to port before the paint was dry. Eight days later, the final weapon came off the line with eighty-nine minutes to spare.

The bazooka went immediately into battle in North Africa. For the soldiers who had never seen them before, it was truly a trial under fire.

Above left: *The soldier holds an anti-tank rocket shell, which is the projectile fired by the bazooka.*

But stories of their success filtered back. When a small coastal fort was giving a landing party considerable trouble, one soldier waded to shore and ended the battle with a single shot. On another occasion, an errant shot from a bazooka struck a tree near a group of six enemy tanks. The startled tank commander surrendered the whole group.

Late in the war, Robert P. Patterson, undersecretary of war, paid a visit to the Bridgeport Works to receive the three hundred thousandth bazooka manufactured by the company. "The Ordnance Department knew what it was doing when it gave the production job to the men and women of this plant . . ." Patterson told the employees. "You did not fail them."

"Oh, We'll Sing of Lydia Pinkham"

Tell me, Lydia, of your secrets,
And the wonders you perform,
How you take the sick and ailing,
And restore them to the norm. . . .
Lizzie Smith had tired feelings,
Terrible pains reduced her weight,
She began to take the Compound,
Now she weighs three hundred and eight.
Elsie W. had no children,
There was nothing in her blouse,
So she took some Vegetable Compound
Now they milk her with the cows.
Oh there's a baby in every bottle,
So the old quotation ran
But the Federal Trade Commission
Still insists you'll need a man.

Lydia E. Pinkham

The Lydia of the song could be none other than Lydia Estes Pinkham, the creator of the famous Lydia E. Pinkham Vegetable Compound that is said to have brought relief from the aches and discomforts of those female ailments that physicians of Pinkham's day deemed normal and natural.

Pinkham never intended to go into business with her cures. She was simply interested in helping women less fortunate

than herself in health. To that end she brewed old-fashioned herb remedies in her kitchen, bottled them, and offered them freely to those in need. Some of the recipes she found in medical books; others had been handed down in her family. Never was a woman turned away from her door without gaining something, if only a cup of fennel tea. And when children came with their mothers, they would each receive a slice of horehound.

When a series of misfortunes left the family destitute, Pinkham's son Dan figured out a solution. "Why not *sell* the Compound? At least to stores!"

Pinkham was shocked at the thought of commercializing on her private charity and immediately answered, "I'd just as soon charge a visitor for a cup of tea!"

But charge she eventually did. Handbills were printed and distributed house to house, first in Lynn, Massachusetts, then Boston, and eventually New York City. Pinkham wrote copy for the handbills, labels for the medicine, and a four-page folder. This forerunner of the modern brochure was entitled *Guide for Women*. Written in a quaintly intimate and highly emotional style, it did much to increase the demand for the Compound.

Business soared. A house was rented next to the Pinkham residence in Lynn and converted into an office and laboratory. To handle the ever-increasing correspondence, Pinkham hired "lady typewriters" and immediately advertised "Remember — all your letters are opened and read in confidence by women. Only women ever had, or ever will have, access to the files. The very office boy is a girl. Even the mailing is done solely by women and girls."

This brought more and more "confidences" and more and more sales.

Top: *Lydia Pinkham's home and laboratory at 233 and 235 Western Avenue, Lynn, Massachusetts. Lydia Pinkham is standing in the doorway at the far right.*
Bottom: *An early advertisement (c. 1886) for Pinkham's Vegetable Compound.*

Do you suffer distress from 'periodic' FEMALE WEAKNESS

With Its Nervous, Highstrung Feelings?

Are you troubled by distress of female functional monthly disturbances? Does it make you feel so nervous, cranky, restless, weak, a bit moody—at such times? Then do try Lydia E. Pinkham's Vegetable Compound to relieve such symptoms! Women by the thousands have reported remarkable benefits.

Pinkham's Compound is what Doctors call a uterine sedative. It has a grand soothing effect on one of woman's most important organs. Taken regularly—Pinkham's Compound helps build up resistance against such distress. It's also a great stomachic tonic! All drugstores.

Change of Life
If the functional 'middle-age' period peculiar to women makes you suffer from hot flashes, weak, highstrung, irritable feelings—try Pinkham's Compound to relieve such symptoms. It's famous for this purpose.

Monthly Female Pains
Pinkham's Compound is very effective to relieve monthly cramps, headache, backache, —when due to female functional monthly disturbances.

Lydia E. Pinkham's VEGETABLE COMPOUND

Pinkham's famous female product was still marketed in the early 1950s.

Dr. Horace Wells

The Lydia E. Pinkham Vegetable Compound is still made today. Of course, the formula has changed somewhat from the original which, it is interesting to note, has never been patented. Nor was there any secrecy about the formula's ingredients. So if you want to whip up your own cure for "all those painful complaints and weaknesses so common to our best female population," here it is:

Lydia Pinkham Vegetable Compound

(with Licorice added for flavoring)   6 ounces Black Cohosh
8 ounces True Unicorn Root   6 ounces Pleurisy Root
8 ounces False Unicorn Root   12 ounces Fenugreek Seed
6 ounces Life Root

"There Shall Be No Pain"

The first painless surgery by the use of ether was performed in 1842 by Dr. Crawford Long. Since the Georgian physician did not publish his results, Dr. Horace Wells, a prominent dentist from Hartford, Connecticut, receives the credit for the discovery of anesthesia. It is not the only strange twist to this story.

On a December evening in 1844, Wells noticed that a man who had inhaled nitrous oxide, or "laughing gas," felt no pain when he injured his leg. Wells wondered if the gas could be used to alleviate the pain of dental surgery. The next night the dentist inhaled nitrous oxide, then allowed a colleague to extract one of his teeth. He felt no pain.

Over the next month, Dr. Wells successfully used nitrous oxide to anesthetize a dozen patients, and in January 1845, he went to Boston to demonstrate his finding at Harvard Medical School. Unfortunately for both Wells and the patient, the gas was withdrawn too quickly, and the patient yelped as his tooth was extracted. Wells felt humiliated, returned to his successful practice in Hartford, and gave up painless dentistry for a time.

In 1846, ether was successfully demonstrated as an anesthetic, leading to a furious debate over who should get the credit for the discovery. Wells went to Paris in 1847 to press his claim before the prestigious medical society of that city. While the controversy bubbled, he opened a painless dentistry practice in New York City.

In January of 1848, the dentist was arrested for throwing acid at a woman walking on Broadway. It was alleged that while under the gas, Wells was transformed into a vicious killer, mainly of young prostitutes,

becoming the original Dr. Jekyll and Mr. Hyde.

Managing to smuggle some chloroform into his cell, he inhaled it and, just before losing consciousness, slashed his femoral artery with a razor. In a suicide note found in his cell, Wells said he had been inhaling chloroform all week for its "exhilarating effect" and had thrown the acid while under the drug's influence. Two weeks later, the Paris Medical Society honored Wells as the first man to discover and use inhaled anesthetics during surgery.

Wells was buried in Cedar Hill Cemetery in Hartford. On his headstone is a bas–relief by Louis Potter titled "There shall be no pain."

The Iron Lung

In 1927, Dr. Philip Drinker, a professor in the School of Public Health at Harvard, watched one day as medical attendants set to work on a young girl with a pulmotor, a bellows-like machine that forced air into failing lungs, then sucked it out again. While the machine saved the little girl's life, she was in obvious pain. It struck Drinker that the theory of mechanically operating the lungs was sound, but the execution was all

Dr. Philip Drinker

The iron lung. The model on the left is an earlier version. Note that in both the patient's head protruded from the apparatus so that food could be taken. Air pressure forced the rhythmic contraction and expansion of the lungs, even when the breathing muscles were paralyzed.

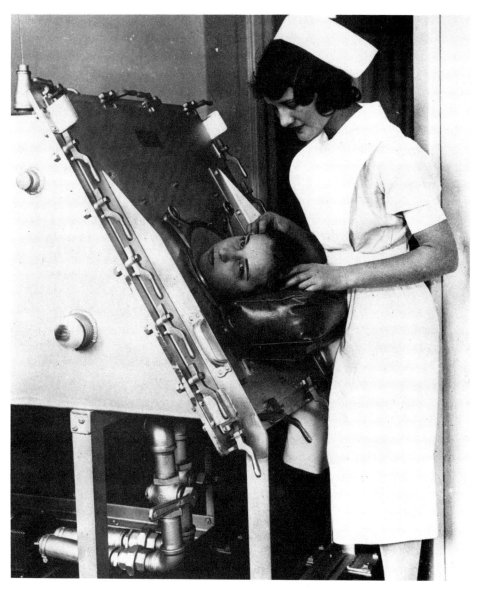

wrong: Rather than pump air into the lungs, the lungs should suck in air, replicating natural breathing.

Earlier, a Swedish physician named Thunberg had experimented with creating a vacuum inside a room; when pressure was applied, the lungs began to work. To Drinker, utilizing an entire room for the purpose of stimulating the lungs was impractical. He decided to build a box big enough to hold a man. Equipped with a pump to alternate vacuum and pressure, the lungs would take in air and then expel it.

The first iron lung was constructed of sheet metal with a vacuum-cleaner blower to draw out the air. A garage dolly served as the bed. When one of Drinker's assistants was fastened in the box, the man's lungs breathed in and out in synch with the motor. Crude and noisy, it worked.

In October of 1928, Drinker had just completed an improved model when a little girl suffering from infantile paralysis was admitted to a Boston hospital. Her lungs were paralyzed. The child was put in the lung and kept alive for several days, until the disease reached her brain.

A second trial was completely successful. A young man was kept in the lung for several weeks, and when he was removed, his lungs had gained enough strength to work on their own.

The Miracle of the Pacemaker

One day in mid-October of 1952, a sixty-five-year-old man walked out of Boston's Beth Israel Hospital following a month-long stay. It was a remarkable occasion, quietly cheered by the international medical community. He was the first individual whose life was saved by a remarkable new device, the external cardiac pacemaker, invented by Dr. Paul Zoll.

A Harvard-educated cardiologist, Zoll began his studies in heart disease while serving in the army during World War II. Dr. Dwight Harken,

MORE PAINLESS DENTISTRY

Yankee dentists have continued the search for painless dentistry ever since Wells. In the early 1970s, Drs. Joseph H. Kronman and Melvin Goldman of Tufts University discovered Caridex, the closest innovation yet to taking the pain out of dentistry since Novocain. The liquid substance, only recently introduced to the market, fragments tooth decay so that it can be scooped out instead of drilled away. Dr. Goldman once proposed a theme song (à la B. B. King), "The Drill Is Gone."

Dr. Paul Zoll shows Mrs. Robert F. Rogers a pacemaker after he was awarded the prestigious Albert Lasker Clinical Medical Research Award. At the time of the photograph in 1973, Mrs. Rogers had lived with a pacemaker implant for twelve years.

207

Dr. Paul Zoll uses a dummy to demonstrate the pacemaker, an electric stimulator, which restarts a heart that has stopped and maintains its normal beat until the heart becomes activated and does the job for itself.

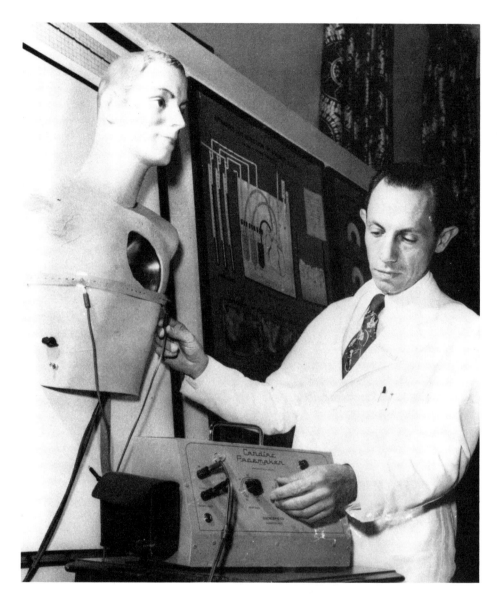

a former classmate of Zoll's, recruited the young physician to his heart team at the 160th General Hospital. There, Harken pioneered the first probes into the heart, removing bullets and shell fragments from wounded soldiers.

As Zoll monitored the electrocardiogram attached to Harken's patients, he was struck by just how tough and resilient the heart actually is. Dr. Claude Beck, a physician at the Cleveland Clinic in Ohio, developed a radical method to resuscitate the heart by cutting open the chest cavity and manually stimulating the heart. But that was a violent maneuver, practical only in life-and-death situations. Zoll was convinced that there must be some rational procedure to reverse heart failure.

"It did seem to me very much too bad that a patient should die of inadequate heart rate or ventricular standstill when the heart is basically so responsive to electrical stimulus," Zoll once said.

Returning to Boston after the war, Zoll first attempted to pass an electrode down the esophagus to stimulate the heart. That soon proved unworkable. In 1952, he came up with an external pacemaker or "shockmaker." A needle was inserted under the skin at the apex of the heart while another electrode was placed on the skin at the fourth rib.

The first clinical test was scheduled for a seventy-five-year-old man who had suffered heart block for two years, but he died before the pacemaker could be tried. Then in September, a sixty-five-year-old man was admitted to the hospital with congestive heart failure. For six days, the man was kept alive with injections of drugs, but the two main pumping chambers of his heart were beating at only half the normal rate. On occasion, his heart stopped for up to a minute.

As all other efforts had failed, the pacemaker was attached. When his heart failed on October 7, the pacemaker took over. For the next fifty-two hours it alone stimulated the heart, sending steady shocks lasting 2/1000ths of a second, fifty to one hundred times a minute. Finally, on October 9, the man's heart began to beat of its own accord. The pacemaker was turned off, and two days later the electrodes were removed. A new age of medicine had arrived.

Gregory
Pincus

"The Pill" Revolution

In 1961, a civil revolt was underway. The unlikely participants were housewives and college girls in states such as Connecticut where it was a clear violation of a law — a criminal misdemeanor — to "use any drug, medical article or instrument for the purpose of preventing conception." Connecticut women were not alone in their disregard for the law: One year after its approval by the FDA, an estimated one million women were "on the pill," and the number was growing by the day.

The search for an oral contraceptive began in early 1951 when Gregory Pincus, cofounder of the Worcester Foundation for Experimental Biology in Shrewsbury, Massachusetts, was visited by Margaret Sanger, founder of Planned Parenthood, and Katherine Dexter McCormick, a widowed heiress. The women asked Pincus how much it would cost to develop a safe, sure method of birth control. When Pincus estimated $125,000, Mrs. McCormick wrote him a check for $40,000 on the spot. The first shot in the pill revolution had just been fired.

Pincus came across an article written some twenty years earlier detailing how progesterone, the female sex hormone, prevented female rabbits from releasing an egg. "If such cycles could be produced at will," the report concluded, "we would have a safe contraceptive method." Since progesterone then cost five thousand dollars an ounce, the study was forgotten.

Things were different in the fifties. Russell Marker, a chemistry professor working in the jungles of Mexico, had invented a way to synthesize progesterone from steroids found in wild yams. Following Marker's discovery, the price of the hormone had dropped to less than fifty cents an ounce. Pincus and his assistants began their experiments with rabbits and rats.

Forty miles away in Brookline, Dr. John Rock was performing similar experiments on women, but for a different purpose. A devout Catholic, Rock was helping women to conceive. By taking large daily doses of progesterone, his patients were able to control their menstrual cycles. Within three or four months after they stopped taking the drug, they became pregnant. While they were taking the drug, they did not ovulate.

Dr. John Rock at his home in Temple, New Hampshire.

After the pair met at a scientific conference, Rock and Pincus decided to join forces. In 1954, Rock began the first human trials of an oral contraceptive with fifty Massachusetts women. The results were promising, but a broader study was needed. There was one catch: Birth control was against the law in Massachusetts. A physician who merely discussed birth control could face a one-thousand-dollar fine and five years in prison. Pincus set up a study at the University of Puerto Rico, and Rock went to the island to act as medical director. They chose a progesterone pill produced by the G.D. Searle Company, Enovid, to use in their tests. Already on the market and used by nearly five hundred thousand women, Enovid was prescribed strictly as a drug to control menstruation.

The Puerto Rican experiments were both a scientific endeavor and a test of public reaction. The island women were devout Catholics, and the church considered birth control a sin. What the doctors found, however, was that poor women clamored to be part of the study — taking the pill, they rationalized, was a sin they could undo. On October 29, 1959, after Rock and Pincus had tested 897 women, G.D. Searle filed its application with the FDA to license the pill for birth control purposes. Seven months later, on May 11, 1960, the pill was approved.

The reaction by women was immediate. By 1965, when a physician at Boston University predicted, "[The pill] will usher in the age of the wanted child," four million women were on the pill, though twenty-five states still strictly regulated or outright banned the sale of contraceptives. Just as immediate was the backlash. Rock was dubbed a "moral rapist" by the Catholic church and was evicted from the building that housed his clinic. Nonetheless, the revolution continued. By 1981, more than seventy million women worldwide practiced birth control with an oral contraceptive.

Looking back, Dr. Rock recalled that it was once a felony to even discuss birth control in the state where the breakthrough occurred. "Life, indeed, has a way . . . of mocking man's more questionable designs," Rock said.

FIRST HOSPITAL USE OF ANESTHESIA

Massachusetts General Hospital in Boston was the first place to use surgical anesthesia. Dr. John Collins Warren removed a tumor from a pioneering patient on October 16, 1846. Afterward, Dr. Collins proudly pronounced, "Gentlemen, this is no humbug."

Artificial Skin

In 1984, Jamie and Glen Selby were removing paint from their naked bodies when the solvent ignited. The Wyoming boys, ages five and six, were both burned over 97 percent of their bodies; the majority of those

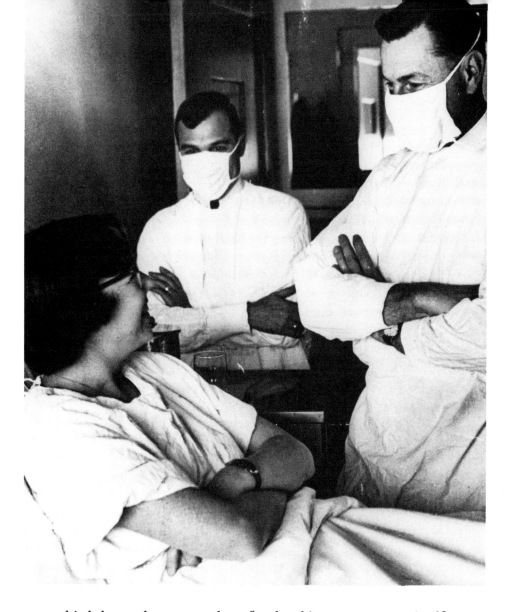

Dr. John Burke (right) talking to a patient. At the time, 1964, he was chairman of the Massachusetts General Hospital Infection Control Committee.

were third-degree burns, too deep for the skin to regenerate itself.

At the Shriners Burn Institute in Boston, small pieces of skin from the boys' armpits were cultured in the laboratory and applied to the wounds. Then the doctors waited to see what would happen.

Not too long ago, the Selbys probably would have died. When severely burned, the rest of the body is susceptible to massive infection and dehydration. Under the best of circumstances, they would have faced a long painful healing process. Thanks to artificial skin, however, Jamie and Glen were back home within fourteen months, and one of them was in school.

Artificial skin was first developed in the 1970s by Dr. John F. Burke, chief of Trauma Services at Boston's Massachusetts General Hospital, and Ioannis V. Yannas, a chemistry professor at MIT. For many years, Burke had been trying to develop a suitable replacement for skin. In late 1969, he was contacted by Yannas, who had studied collagen, the protein that largely composes skin. Collaborating, the two discovered that collagen fibers are found in the skin together with another structure called GAG. By taking collagen from readily available sources, such as cowhide, and combining it with GAG, the new substance could be treated to form a supple, porous material that encouraged growth of healthy skin cells around it. In 1975, the first tests were conducted on guinea pigs; the test wounds appeared to heal successfully.

GAG for the skin was extracted from shark cartilage and blended into a solution of collagen extracted from cowhide. The new skin was freeze-dried, baked, and sterilized into a synthetic material with two layers as soft, pliable, and sensitive as the real thing: The top layer, or epidermis, was made of silicone; the bottom, or dermis, was derived from the cowhide and shark cartilage. After twenty-seven days, the outer silicone layer, which acts as a temporary protective coating, is removed.

The first critical human test occurred in 1979. A young woman was rushed to Massachusetts General Hospital with burns covering nearly 60 percent of her body. After the burned skin was stripped away, artificial skin was applied. Three weeks later, when doctors examined the wounds, they found new tissue full of life. Portions of the woman's unburned skin were spread widely over her body to create a permanent layer of new skin. Within three weeks, the new skin was approximately the same color as her unburned skin.

Since then the process has been refined, improved, and pushed for-

Dr. John F. Burke

213

ward. At Harvard Medical School, Dr. Howard Green developed the procedure to grow sheets of epidermis in the lab from a piece of patient skin the size of a postage stamp. And Burke and Yannas are developing a membrane that will cover the wound and let it change over to natural skin without any more treatment. "We've stepped into a bigger room, which is also dark," Burke once told a reporter from *Reader's Digest.* "But that just means we have to light another candle."

A Clone Is a Clone Is a Clone . . .

On January 15, 1979, a short article with a long title appeared in the *American Journal of Obstetrics and Gynecology.* The author of "Diploid Nuclear Replacement in Mature Human Ova with Cleavage," was Landrum B. Shettles, M.D., Ph.D., one of the world's leading authorities on human reproduction and a physician at the Gifford Memorial Hospital in Randolph, Vermont. The article described Shettles's successful efforts to remove the nucleus from a mature human egg and replace it with the nucleus of a cell taken from male tissue. Having achieved the transfer with delicate microsurgery, Shettles then put the eggs in a lab vessel containing nutrients essential for their growth. The eggs divided and in three days reached the multi-cellular stage of development at

Dr. Shettles, a pioneer in the field of reproductive biology, is especially proud of his microphotographs of developing human eggs and embryos.

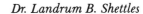
Dr. Landrum B. Shettles

which a normally fertilized egg makes its home in the womb.

That was as far as the experiment went. The embryos eventually stopped dividing and died. But, as Shettles wrote in his article, "There was every indication that each specimen was developing normally and could readily have been transferred 'in utero,' " that is, to a human womb or uterus.

Had he done so, and had one of those embryos grown into a baby and been born, Dr. Shettles would have achieved two breathtaking feats — the baby would have been the first "test-tube" baby born in the United States, and it would have been genetically identical to the donor of the male cell nucleus. In short, it would have been a carbon copy of a living thing — a single-parent child — a clone.

It was just the kind of experiment that both thrilled and horrified Shettles's contemporaries. Ten years earlier, some of his colleagues disputed Shettles's claim to have achieved the first steps toward test-tube conception. In 1973, he resigned from his post at the Columbia-Presbyterian Medical Center when his efforts to achieve test-tube fertilization for a Florida dentist and his wife who could not conceive naturally were discovered. Shettles was accused of "trying to create a monster." Eventually he moved to Vermont.

The experiment in cloning raised the same kind of hackles from medical ethicists who disputed Shettles's claims, and argued that cloning was a threat to human individuality. ". . . [F]iddle around, if you must fiddle," Dr. Lewis Thomas, author of *Lives of a Cell,* advised, "but never with ways to keep things the same. Heaven, somewhere ahead, has got to be a change."

Shettles said his work was simply driven by curiosity. "I was just probing, trying to see what I could find," he explained. "I guess I was a little bit too naive to think about the implications of it . . . . [I]f I did a wrong thing, it was not intentionally."

Of Mice, Men, and Genes

When Nobel Prize-winner Dr. George Snell of Bar Harbor, Maine, was starting out in cancer research, fifty or so years ago, medicine's hottest quest was to determine why some people get cancer and others don't. Researchers experimenting with animals would cut out a piece of a mouse's tumor, scissor off a fragment, and insert it under the skin of a healthy mouse. While most times the recipient mouse would remain healthy, often enough a hapless beast would "catch" the cancer.

Dr. George Snell, chatting with his wife Rhoda after winning the Nobel Prize for medicine, in 1980.

Why? And why not every time? The answer soon came clear and was surprisingly simple. A tumor is body tissue gone crazy reproducing itself — but tissue nevertheless, so it behaves like tissue. Doctors knew, even in 1935, that skin grafts and other tissue transplants were rejected by a patient unless the donor was the patient's identical twin or related to the recipient through a high degree of inbreeding. What they didn't know was how the recipient *knows* what is alien and what is "as though of itself."

When 32-year-old George Snell showed up in 1935 for a new job at Bar Harbor's Jackson Laboratory, then a small institution staffed by mouse geneticists, he undertook to identify the batch of genes, probably located on different chromosomes, that appeared to control the acceptance or rejection of a transplant.

In 1935, when the electron microscope was not yet invented, nobody had ever seen a gene. Snell had to go about his quest for the "invisible" in a most tedious, yet ingenious way. He undertook to inbreed families of mice by mating, remating, and backmating progeny with their brothers and sisters, even their parents, for generations, then transplanting tumors from one to another. Mice, born about ten to a litter, can mate six weeks after birth and require only three weeks to gestate. Thus a single pair can multiply to five generations and hundreds of descendants in a year. Meticulously recording thousands upon thousands of births and acceptance or rejection of each tumor, Snell, working alone except for hired feeders and waterers, inbred his mice for similarity until their family trees amounted to whole races of almost identical "twins."

Almost. Actually, Snell set out to develop family trees not in single groups but in pairs. Mice in one family tree of a pair would be genetically identical to mice in the other family tree except for one gene: One family strain would refuse to accept transplants from the other, even though they were, in other ways, genetic "twins." Such pairings of strains differing by only one gene are called "congenic." Thus Snell began to isolate, in congenic strains of mice, the acceptance/rejection gene (or genes) he was looking for. Snell calculated that creating the founding parents of each strain of such remarkable mice took fourteen generations of controlled inbreeding.

Even so, how could he hope to identify which genes, among the mouse's countless combinations, were the actual ones that said "yes" or "no" to transplants? For this too he had a plan — he would look for "markers."

From the beginning, Snell surmised that the genes determining acceptance or rejection also had other functions. They might, for example, help determine whether or not a mouse was to have purple eyes or an inside-out belly button. Sure enough. Snell soon discovered that any two mice with fused tails always accepted one another's transplants. So the instruction for fused tails and for transplant acceptance must come from genes closely linked on the same chromosome. Fused tails became one of the markers — *visible* markers — for the invisible characteristic of transplant acceptance. Other markers soon turned up.

Fascinating, glamorous work, eh? Fascinating, perhaps, but glamorous, no. Every night after work, Snell had to change his clothes to protect

Dr. George Snell, posing with a "Jax" mouse, famed for its role in medical and genetic research.

218

his family from mouse odors. And there was the tedium, crossing after crossing of mouse relatives for generation after generation, year after year, separating the tumor "takes" from the rejections, then mating the mice again while records of family trees proliferated.

Snell eventually came to the breakthrough genetic discovery that would win him world recognition. Patience, vigilance, clarity of method, and purpose — those were the qualities of mind that led Snell to his goal; his was not an "Aha!" like the accidental discovery of penicillin. While specifically identifying and locating as many as twelve genes that control aspects of acceptance or rejection of foreign donations, Snell discovered a single cluster of genes exercising central command over the "decisions" of the others. Some scientists have dubbed this cluster "super gene." More formally Snell called it the "major histocompatibility complex."

Before long, one of Snell's cowinners of the Nobel Prize, Dr. Jean Dausset of Paris, established that a similar gene complex exists in humans. These discoveries formed a foundation of subsequent and still ongoing research in transplanting organs, in immunizing against disease, even in identifying a child's father in a paternity suit.

A method for proving paternity, even as a minor research byproduct, was scarcely what Snell had in mind when he embarked on his long quest. In fact, Snell wasn't quite sure just what his target was. That's often the case when a scientist sets out on a course of "pure" or "basic" research. "I knew I was gambling," Snell says today, "and you have to have some luck when you gamble. The best I could do when I started was to see a path I could follow. That's the most important part in basic research: not the practical goal, but just seeing your direction when you begin."

INDEX

PICTURE CREDITS

CHAPTER THREE: pp. 51 bottom, 52: Pat D'Amato. p. 53: top, courtesy Sherman Howe; bottom, The Vermont Historical Society. pp. 54, 56, 57: The National Baseball Library, Cooperstown, NY. p. 58: top, Marc Peloquin; bottom, The Basketball Hall of Fame. p. 59 (both): Courtesy The Basketball Hall of Fame. p. 60: The Bettmann Archive. p. 61 (both): Courtesy The Volleyball Hall of Fame, Holyoke, MA. p. 62: The Bettmann Archive. p. 63 left: Culver Pictures, Inc. p. 64 right: From *The Book of Candlepin Bowling.* p. 65: Plimoth Plantation. p. 66: bottom and left, courtesy Worcester Historical Society; right, courtesy Gallery Collections. p. 67: top left, courtesy Worcester Historical Society; top right, courtesy Gallery Collections; bottom right, courtesy Elizabeth Plimpton. p. 68: Culver Pictures, Inc. p. 69: left, Culver Pictures, Inc.; right, courtesy *Golf* magazine. p. 70: top, Carole Allen; bottom, Craig MacCormack. p. 71 (both): Courtesy General Electric. p. 72: Courtesy Bridgeport Public Library. pp. 73, 74: Courtesy Milton Bradley. p. 75: top, courtesy Philips/Magnavox; bottom, Wide World Photos.

CHAPTER FOUR: p. 78 bottom: Courtesy The Boston Public Library, Print Department. p. 79 bottom and left: Northeast Archives of Folklore, University of Maine, Orono. p. 80: The Bostonian Society p. 82: Composite from a photograph from The Bettmann Archive. p. 83: Courtesy Ocean Spray Cranberries, Inc. p. 86: University of Illinois Communications Library, Champaign-Urbana. p. 87: The Bostonian Society. p. 88: top, Doug Mindell; bottom, University of Illinois Communications Library, Champaign-Urbana. p. 89 left: Courtesy Woodman's. p. 90: top, courtesy The Boston Public Library, Print Department; bottom, Doug Mindell. p. 91: Courtesy Mrs. Nina Donatello. pp. 92–94: Courtesy Bowers and Merena Galleries, Inc., Box 1224, Wolfeboro, NH. p. 95: Courtesy Public Affairs Office, US Army, Natick, MA.

CHAPTER FIVE: p. 97 bottom: The Connecticut Historical Society, Hartford. p. 98 bottom: The Bettmann Archive. p. 99 top: The Bettmann Archive. p. 100 bottom: University of Illinois Communications Library, Champaign-Urbana. p. 101: From *The Branding of America,* courtesy The Butterick Company. pp. 102 top, 103 top: Archives, Shaker Village, Inc., Canterbury,

NH. p. 105: top, Wide World Photos; bottom, University of Illinois Communications Library, Champaign-Urbana. p. 106: University of Illinois Communications Library, Champaign-Urbana. p. 107: top, University of Illinois Communications Library, Champaign-Urbana; bottom, courtesy Amana Refrigeration Inc. p. 108 right: Courtesy Amana Refrigeration Inc. p. 109 bottom: Courtesy *Yankee Homes.* p. 110: Courtesy *Yankee Homes.* p. 111: Yale University Library. p. 112 (both): Courtesy The Gerald R. Ford Library. pp. 113, 114: Courtesy The Boston Public Library, Print Department. p. 115: Wide World Photos.

CHAPTER SIX: pp. 118, 119, 120 top: From *The Atlantic Cable* by Bern Dibner, courtesy The Burndy Library, Inc., Norwalk, CT. pp. 120 bottom and 121: Culver Pictures, Inc. p. 122 top right and bottom: Culver Pictures, Inc. p. 123 top right: Culver Pictures, Inc. p. 124 (both): The Bettmann Archive. p. 125: top, The Bettmann Archive; bottom, Culver Pictures, Inc. p. 126: Courtesy The Wadsworth Atheneum, Hartford. pp. 127, 128 top: Courtesy The Wadsworth Atheneum, Hartford. Gift of Benjamin and Paul Cooley. pp. 128 bottom, 129, 130 top: Courtesy L.L. Bean. pp. 130 bottom, 131 bottom: Courtesy The Fuller Brush Company. p. 131 margin: University of Illinois Communications Library, Champaign-Urbana. p. 133 top: Courtesy The Fuller Brush Company. pp. 133–135: Courtesy Tupperware Home Parties, Inc.

CHAPTER SEVEN: p. 137: The Bettmann Archive. pp. 138, 139 bottom, 140: Courtesy The Mark Twain Memorial, Hartford. p. 142 top: Courtesy The Worcester Historical Museum. pp. 142 bottom, 143 and 144 top: Courtesy Samuel Cabot, Inc. pp. 146 bottom and 147 top: The Collections of The Maine Historical Society. p. 147 bottom: Culver Pictures, Inc. pp. 148, 149: From the collection of Keith Marvin, The Bennington Museum. pp. 150, 151: Yankee Archives, courtesy Bartlett Gould. p. 152 bottom: Archives of American Art, Smithsonian Institution, from *Rufus Porter Rediscovered* by Jean Lipman, Clarkson N. Potter Publishers, 1980. p. 153: Culver Pictures, Inc. p. 154 top: The Smithsonian Institution, photo # A18792. p. 154 bottom: Wide World Photos. p. 155: Courtesy Boone T. Guyton. pp. 156, 157 top: Courtesy Bartlett Gould. pp. 158, 159: Everett "Red" Boutiller.

CHAPTER EIGHT: p. 161: Courtesy Marjorie Winchenpaw/Cote Photography. p. 162: Courtesy Deb Hunter. pp. 163, 164 top: The Rhode Island Historical Society. pp. 165–167: The American Morgan Horse Museum. p. 168: Courtesy the collection of Nancy Cowan. p. 169: Courtesy Harry Gray. p. 170 top: Courtesy Lawrence Orne. pp. 171, 172 bottom: Ivan Massar. pp. 173, 174: Courtesy Lee Fairchild. p. 175 top: Doug Mindell. pp. 176, 177 top: Lawrence Willard. p. 178 top: Courtesy Gretchen Poisson. p. 179 bottom: Lawrence Willard. p. 180: Courtesy Dr. Walton Galinat. p. 181 (both): Peter Vandermark.

CHAPTER NINE: p. 184 left: *The Hartford Courant.* p. 185 bottom: The Bostonian Society. p. 187: Craig MacCormack. p. 188: Yankee Archives. p. 189 bottom: Culver Pictures, Inc. p. 190 (both): The Boston Public Library, Print Department. p. 191: Yankee Archives. p. 192 left: Wide World Photos. pp. 192 right, 193: The Bettmann Archive.

CHAPTER TEN: p. 195: Yale University Library. p. 196: top, The Bettmann Archive; bottom, courtesy The Connecticut State Library. pp. 197, 198: The Bettmann Archive. p. 199 top: Courtesy The Connecticut State Library. p. 199 bottom: The Bettmann Archive. pp. 200, 201 left: Courtesy General Electric. pp. 202, 203 top: Yankee Archives. p. 203 bottom: Culver Pictures, Inc. p. 204: top, Yankee Archives; bottom, Culver Pictures, Inc. p. 205 top: Culver Pictures, Inc. pp. 205 bottom, 206 left: Harvard University Archives. p. 206 right: The Bettmann Archive. p. 207 bottom: Wide World Photos. pp. 208, 209: The Bettmann Archive. p. 210: Wide World Photos. p. 211: The Bostonian Society. p. 212: The Boston Public Library, Print Department. p. 213: Wide World Photos. pp. 214, 215: Lawrence Willard. p. 216: Wide World Photos. p. 218: Carole Allen.